dati...

BASIC
TRAINING

chris and adrienne
PLEKENPOL

In-Him Publishing
4020 N. MacArthur Blvd. #122-320 Irving, TX 75038

Dating Basic Training
Copyright © 2011 by Chris and Adrienne Plekenpol

Cover illustration by Can Photo Stock
Cover Design by Chris Plekenpol

Unless otherwise indicated, Scripture quotations are from:
The Holy Bible, New International Version (NIV 1984) by International
Bible Society used by permission.
The Message by Eugene H. Peterson
© 1993, 1994, 1995, 1996, 2000, 2001, 2002
Used by permission of NavPress Publishing Group
New American Standard Bible®, copyright 1960, 1962, 1963, 1968, 1971,
1972, 1973,1975, 1977, 1995 by the Lockman Foundation. Used by per-
mission.

For More Information:
www.datingbasictraining.com
www.chrisplekenpol.com

Library of Congress Cataloging-in Publication Data
Plekenpol, Chris
Plekenpol, Adrienne
Dating Basic Training /Chris and Adrienne Plekenpol.
    p. 196
ISBN-13: 978-1466402256
ISBN-10: 1466402253
12 11 10 / 6 5 4 3 2 1

TABLE OF CONTENTS

Acknowledgments		5
Section One:	Introduction	7
Section Two:	The Way Things Ought To Be	11
Chapter 1:	Adam and Eve	13
Chapter 2:	Jesus on Genesis	21
Chapter 3:	Marriage and Singleness	25
Chapter 4:	Christian Submission	41
Section Three:	The Way Things Are	49
Chapter 5:	Broken Marriages	53
Chapter 6:	Cohabitation	57
Chapter 7:	Facing Dating Realities	59
Chapter 8:	Dating Types to Avoid	63
Section Four:	Descriptive, Not Prescriptive Dating	69
Chapter 9:	Isaac and Rebekah	71
Chapter 10:	Jacob and Rachel (and Leah)	79
Chapter 11:	Boaz and Ruth	85
Chapter 12:	David and Abigail	93
Chapter 13:	Solomon and the Shulamite	97
Chapter 14:	Samson and the Philistines	109
Section Five:	Prescriptive Dating	117
Chapter 15:	The Search	119
Chapter 16:	Must Be a Believer	133
Chapter 17:	How	137
Chapter 18:	Give Me Steps	145
Chapter 19:	Dating the Divorced	153
Section Six:	Appendix (Examples)	161
Notes		194

ACKNOWLEDGEMENTS

We want to thank God for the grace to write this book. It has been a process of living, failing, and letting God work through us. Thank you, Jesus for never leaving us, even when we felt our worst and didn't deserve your presence or your grace. We're learning more and more what a real friend You are.

We want to thank our moms for investing in us to help us get this book out to the public. We want to thank our dads who have been instrumental in helping and encouraging us.

Jennifer Carpenter, Adrienne's mom, thank you so much for taking time to edit and give us your time and your contructive criticism. This would never have made it beyond a good idea without that.

Jenna Warner, our cousin, thanks for the help on the editing and your perspective, wisdom, and warnings. They were exactly what we needed.

We want to thank the college students at the University of North Texas, Dallas Baptist University, the University of Oklahoma, the University of Texas, Texas A&M, the United States Military Academy at West Point, the University of Southern California, and a host of other schools that have let us get into your lives and help navigate you through the triumphs and heartaches which are relationships.

section one

INTRODUCTION

When I was in high school, and I told people I was going into the army, people laughed. They couldn't conceive of me, the most free-spirited person on the planet, ever submitting myself to something so regimented. I laughed it off. I had been yelled at before growing up in sports. I figured that I would just get there and let any correction roll off my back.

I arrived at West Point and received a rude awakening. I couldn't believe how hard it was. I had never been trained. I didn't have any idea how to interact with military people. I was completely clueless.

I needed training. And that is how I wanted to write this book—from a training angle.

I know that ladies are reading this book as well, and perhaps the military inuendos aren't helping you at all. So for you, let me use a slightly different theme in each section: dancing.

I have three rules when I walk out on a dance floor. Rule number one: the man is in charge. Some say dancing is the last bastion of male chauvinism. Maybe, but no matter if you are a social conservative or liberal, you can't argue the fact that there are no dances created that have a female lead. So like it or not, unless the man initiates the dance, nobody moves.

Rule number two is the woman is never at fault. Her job is to respond to the man's initiative. I know what you're thinking. There are some women who have absolutely no rhythm. They have no capacity to dance. How can the woman not be at fault? The man is the one who initiated the dance. It's his problem for continuing dancing with a woman who has no ability or capacity to dance. The smart thing for that man to do is stop dancing with her. Find someone else. That might sound harsh, but when I go to dance, I'm not looking to make someone feel good. I'm looking to dance.

Rule number three is the whole purpose of the dance is to make the woman look good. If the woman looks good, then the couple looks good.

If there is one thing that will get a young person's full attention— it's relationships. Relationships dominate the landscape of student life and beyond for those that are single. Hollywood and the media have portrayed the marriage ceremony as the pinnacle of life. We bought it—at least I did. I know this is crazy, but throughout my college years at West Point, all my spare time was caught up in trying to find the one. I tried it all. I let my parents set me up. I tried dating websites. I tried engaging with every woman possible. The weird thing was none of them were the one. I went to the ends of the earth searching and looking and pleading at times with God to bring me a spouse. It wasn't until I accepted Christ that I even began to understand that only God is the ultimate thing.

When I became a Christian I wanted to learn how to approach women appropriately. However, I didn't seek out any men in my life to guide me through the process. I think a lot of guys are like that. We view American fathers as great teachers of how to throw a baseball so we don't look like a girl, but sometimes we are afraid to look to them in the area of relational development. And for many American men that are now on their own and single, what do you do when you can't talk to your dad about those things?

Personally, I spent the next twelve years fumbling through dating. I tried to kiss dating goodbye and failed at that miserably. It was a weird social experiment gone bad. I tried running hard toward

God, looking to my left and right to see who was running with me. I found I wasn't interested in any of those women. In fact no one seemed to be the *one*.

I ended up getting married at age 34. I now find myself counseling countless young people through the same rough waters I tried to navigate alone. I wanted to put together a book with my wife to give a little more direction to those who are trailblazing the path of relationships. I want to use the Bible as our guide and explain tradition, culture, and other things that make us who we are—the good, the bad, and the ugly.

Here is the weird part about me (and I have told my wife this), I didn't marry the *one*. I became the *one*. Don't take that in an arrogant way. Becoming the *one* was not some super spiritual plane, but a realization that God never intended our spouses to be our ultimate "American Dream" fulfillment which screams, "I love me!" He intended us to live as one so that when we looked into the eyes of our spouse we don't say, "I love you," but rather say, "I love me," embracing the truth that the two have become *one*.

This book contains real stories from real people. To keep all of those whom I know sane and not searching for themselves or others, I have changed the names and mixed up the situations to prevent those whom I love from trying to figure out who is who—which will probably happen anyway.

section two

THE WAY THINGS OUGHT TO BE

Being a soldier is simple. The fundamental training is never hard. Being a military strategist is not required. It helps, but even that can be learned. A soldier learns how to shoot, move, and communicate on the battlefield from day one. Learning how to handle adversity is something that every soldier must learn or face defeat.

I remember training my soldiers how to kick in a door and take a building in 20 degree weather in the middle of the night in Colorado. We trained so that the men could take a building without thinking. After making mistakes over and over, they eventually learned how to take the building with no problem. It took training. It took young soldiers listening to older soldiers explain to them in a very direct manner how to do their job.

Rifle marksmanship was the same way. We took boys who didn't know what an M-4 was from a .22 and turned them into expert riflemen.

In combat, men needed the training. When they got complacent, bad things happened. Peoples lives were forever changed for the worse.

Dating is no different.

Dancing is simple. The fundamental moves are never hard. Rhythm is not a requirement. It helps, but even that can be learned. *Dancing with the Stars* proves anyone can dance. Given a Broadway dance star, a professional dance instructor, and a couple of weeks of training, anyone can do it.

Amongst all the flash, cool dresses, and crazy moves, are basic steps. These steps don't change. They are the same for everyone. The waltz, for example, can be performed counter-clockwise around the outside of the ballroom or can be performed using the basic box step. The waltz requires a ¾ timing and utilizes the rise and fall rhythm, while performing the basic step and any variations. When most people read that, they do a patronizing nod and move on. For those who have taken dance lessons, this isn't quite so tough. In fact, it is something they can easily visualize.

However, the point I'm trying to make is that no one is born knowing how to dance. It's an art and a science. The ¾ timing of the waltz never changes. The rest is played out on the dance floor. You can have waltz music but be in ¼ timing. You are no longer doing a dance, but looking like an idiot and probably bumping into a lot of people.

Dating is no different.

I want to restore some sense of decency to the dance floor, at least among Christians. We of all people should be showing the non-believing world what this should look like. But for most of us, no one taught us how.

God had a plan for people and relationships. He had it diagrammed out. From the creation of Adam and Eve, God put people in relationship with one another. Adam and Eve didn't exactly put the human race in position for success.

God wasn't left wringing his hands wondering how this would all work out. He gave us His Word.

chapter one:

ADAM AND EVE

What do you think about when you think about Adam and Eve? I usually think about an apple, a tree, a snake, and them ruining the entire human race.

"Don't eat the forbidden fruit!" isn't the only lesson that God can teach us through Adam and Eve.

Let's walk through their story and learn how it all began.

Genesis 2:18		
NASV	NIV	NET
Then the LORD God said, "It is not good for the man to be alone; I will make him a **helper suitable** for him."	The LORD God said, "It is not good for the man to be alone. I will make a **helper suitable** for him."	The LORD God said, "It is not good for the man to be alone. I will make a **companion** for him who **corresponds** to him."

Observation/Interpretation:

Creation wasn't complete when Adam was single. Many well intentioned people have said things like, "All you need is God. Stop looking for a spouse." That statement is hurtful. You may not need a spouse, but God said that Adam alone was not good. He needed to create a helper or companion for him. You may be called to singleness, but you are never called to be alone.

From the Hebrew word "ezer" we get the word *helper*, but it does not mean solely *helper*. The New English Translation translated "ezer" as *companion* because the English word *helper* can have many different ideas and meanings. It does not accurately convey the full definition of the Hebrew word "ezer." Usage of the Hebrew term does not suggest a subordinate role, a connotation which English "helper" can have.

In the Bible, God is frequently described as *helper*, the one who does for us what we cannot do for ourselves. He is the one who meets our needs. In this context the word seems to express the idea of an indispensable companion. The woman would supply what the man was lacking in the design of creation. It would follow that the man would supply what she was lacking, although that is not stated here.

I like this. It eases our minds and worries, especially if you come from a less-than-traditional home, where perhaps the mother works and might even be the primary bread winner.

God looked over his creation and said something wasn't good. I had at times wondered if perhaps God made a mistake. Perhaps one day he was pairing up all the animals. He looked at Adam and said, "Ah crud! I knew I forgot something." I don't think it is divine forgetfulness, but rather a mark on humanity that we are better together than we are alone.

Genesis 2:19-20	
NASV	NET
Out of the ground the LORD God formed every beast of the field and every bird of the sky, and brought them to the man to see what he would call them; and whatever the man called a living creature, that was its name. The man gave names to all the cattle, and to the birds of the sky, and to every beast of the field, but for Adam there was not found a **helper suitable** for him.	The LORD God formed out of the ground every living animal of the field and every bird of the air. He brought them to the man to see what he would name them, and whatever the man called each living creature, that was its name. So the man named all the animals, the birds of the air, and the living creatures of the field, but for Adam no **companion** who **corresponded** to him was found.

Observation/Interpretation:

Adam actively searched for a companion through what God had put on earth. Weird, right? Adam was out looking for a companion. He was actively searching. It's odd that he wasn't looking among humans, but he was looking, all the same. God knew Adam was looking and hadn't found anyone, yet God allowed him to look anyway.

I can relate. In my search for a wife, I often felt like that. "Hey God, I know you're sovereign and all. You know that I need a companion. I am looking for a companion/helper, but you aren't providing a companion/helper—what gives?"

Genesis 2:21-22

So the LORD God caused the man to fall into a deep sleep; and while he was sleeping, he took one of the man's ribs and closed up the place with flesh. Then the LORD God made a woman from the rib he had taken out of the man, and he brought her to the man.

Observation/Interpretation:

This woman was to be a helpmate. We aren't here to argue

equality or roles in marriage. It is clear from the New Testament that the woman in marriage comes under the authority of the man. God brought Eve to Adam to make for Adam what paradise couldn't provide.

At the beginning of the sentence there is the transitional word *so*. In the Hebrew this is a *waw* pronounced, "vav." A transitional word goes along with a transitional statement, which is a sentence that hinges on the previous sentence. In this case the previous sentence is, "For Adam no suitable helper or companion was found."

We bring that point up because God and Adam are both looking for a suitable helper/companion. They can't find one. So, to fix the problem, God puts Adam into a deep sleep, takes out a rib, and forms Eve around the rib. This could be the first and only example of successful human DNA cloning. Perhaps this leads us to see that only God should clone—but we won't go there.

Picture for a moment the last wedding you saw. The father of the bride with loving eyes and a tender touch gently makes a last-minute fix to his daughter's veil. He remembers her as a little girl and now can't believe he's giving her away. He peers through the little window of the double doors leading into the sanctuary and sees the man to whom he will give his daughter. He is giving her away to him.

You may not know it, but we do this traditionally to represent what God the Father did when he gave Eve to Adam. This is the perfect picture of "the Lord brought her to the man."

God partners with man to find his mate.

There is a selection process, but this does not mean that there is only one mate hand-crafted by God for the man, but rather that man is not compatible with animals. This rules out bestiality.

Some take this as God has only one option for a spouse seeker. Each man has one woman perfectly designed for him. Reality check. The first thing that Eve did as this "perfect helpmate woman" was let the serpent deceive her. Adam violated rule number one by abdicating his position of leadership. We have two people in paradise whom God without doubt made for one another. Immediately the perfect couple, who a moment before were naked and unashamed, were now hacking up fig branches to cover up their privates. Meanwhile, they have unwittingly led all of mankind into depravity.

God may ask you to take a nap while walking with him in the cool of the day. He then might rip a rib out of you and bring you a woman. You will know for sure she's *the one*.

Now one could formulate the principle that God created *the one* for you, and it is man's job to find her. There is a specific woman for every man. But that is not the point of this scripture. This process just eliminated animals as a helpmate. Since there wasn't a woman, God made one.

I already see these questions rising. Didn't God create Eve for Adam? Yes. Here is the question I will ask you. When did Adam know Eve was *the one*? He didn't see God forming her. He didn't even see God bringing her to him. He just woke up one day and was married—kinda how it is for a lot of guys actually.

Is there one person you are supposed to marry? Yes. You will know who that is, however, after God has joined you together at the altar.

If you could only marry one specific person, then our whole world order would be in big trouble. Think about it. If one person married the wrong person (God checked out of being sovereign for a while), it would destroy the whole human race.

Here is what I mean. If instead of marrying Adrienne, I married Lisa, then Adrienne would have no choice but to marry the wrong one. She marries Mike. Well, clearly Mike wasn't the right one and so *the one* Mike was supposed to marry, Helen, is now stuck with Bob. Do you see how that goes?

You may subscribe to the fact that you are either called to marry *the one* or stay single. I can handle that at least rationally, because by not marrying *the one*, you don't wreck the human race. The problem is everyone else would. How would you know if you married the right one? How would you know that you were supposed to marry Helen or remain a confirmed bachelor?

I get nervous just thinking about it.

You were meant to marry one person, but you will only know who that is after you say, "I do."

Back to Genesis.

Genesis 2:23-25 (NIV)
 The man said,
  "This is now bone of my bones
  and flesh of my flesh;
 she shall be called 'woman,'
  for she was taken out of man."
 That is why a man leaves his father and mother and is
united to his wife, and they become one flesh.
 Adam and his wife were both naked, and they felt no
shame.

Observation/Interpretation:
 God brought Adam this new creature who was similar to him, but
different. Adam called her *ishah*, a name very similar to *ish*, the word
for man. He looked at his wife and recognized that she was from
him and for him. The next thing that Moses wrote about was the
fact that they became one flesh. One flesh—what a strange thought.
God took from the man a rib. From that rib He made a completely
new person—not so that he could have two different people.
 He wanted the two to function as one. Hello, hot steamy sex.
There is a oneness when the man penetrates the woman. They are
one connected body. There is a companionship oneness where they
are "joined at the hip." There is an emotional oneness when they
"are of one mind." They know each other deeply, and there is no
judgment or shame. There is nothing hidden between them physically, emotionally, or spiritually. The two become one.
 So here it is. When a man and woman marry, the man no longer looks at another person. He looks at the other half of himself.
When a woman marries a man, she no longer looks at another person. She looks at the other half of herself. He no longer says, "I love
you," but rather, "I love me."

APPLICATION

- You partner with God to find a mate.

It is Biblical and righteous for man to search for a mate. There is a dynamic of God's approval involved in selecting a spouse. God designed marriage to best work with the man as leader and the woman as his helper and companion.

- You should never worry about marrying *the one*.

The one exists only after God has made the two *one*.

chapter two:
JESUS ON GENESIS

Jesus was constantly being set up by those who weren't too thrilled by his popularity. Good for us, He always knew He was being set up in a verbal trap. He used the conversation to teach a timeless truth. You remember the story in Matthew 19. Jesus was doing His thing, healing people and making religious people furious. The religious people come up to Jesus with this question to test Him. They asked, "Is it lawful for a man to divorce his wife for any and every reason?"

Matthew 19:4-9 (NIV)

"Haven't you read," Jesus replied, "that at the beginning the Creator 'made them male and female,' and said, 'For this reason a man will leave his father and mother and be united to his wife, and the two will become one flesh'? So they are no longer two, but one flesh. Therefore what God has joined together, let no one separate."

"Why then," they asked, "did Moses command that a man give his wife a certificate of divorce and send her away?"

Jesus replied, "Moses permitted you to divorce your wives because your hearts were hard. But it was not this way from the beginning. I tell you that anyone who divorces his wife, except for sexual immorality, and marries another woman commits adultery."

Observation/Interpretation:

Jesus believed that there was one woman meant for one man. The only way one will know who her spouse was meant to be is after God has joined the two together together.

Notice Jesus referred to the fact that during the time of Moses, women were being discarded as if yesterday's trash. To protect women so that they could marry again and be taken care of, God allowed Moses to give women a certificate of divorce.

In that day, there wasn't exactly a choice in who you married. Your parents brought you a spouse, and you got married. This is what God said on the issue in Deuteronomy:

Deuteronomy 24:1-4 (NIV)

If a man marries a woman who becomes displeasing to him because he finds something indecent about her, and he writes her a certificate of divorce, gives it to her and sends her from his house, and if after she leaves his house she becomes the wife of another man, and her second husband dislikes her and writes her a certificate of divorce, gives it to her and sends her from his house, or if he dies, then her first husband, who divorced her, is not allowed to marry her again after she has been defiled.

That would be detestable in the eyes of the LORD. Do not bring sin upon the land the LORD your God is giving you as an inheritance.

The disciples and everyone else operated on what Moses said. Sure, they thought what God said in Genesis 2 was great, but the reality was that women were hard to deal with. Rabbis, in that time, debated what qualified as displeasing to the man. Some argued it was adultery only, and others argued it could be as simple as burning his dinner.

Perhaps some felt that if a man couldn't divorce his wife, the woman might have some power over the hard-luck man. The culture of Jerusalem and their view of women wasn't too different from what we have depicted today in our media. Billboards, magazines, and TV portray a woman as here to please her man. And if she doesn't—away with her. The disciples knew themselves. Their dark hearts confessed freely in Matthew 19.

Matthew 19:10-12 (NIV)
> The disciples said to him, "If this is the situation between a husband and wife, it is better not to marry."
> Jesus replied, "Not everyone can accept this word, but only those to whom it has been given. For there are eunuchs who were born that way, and there are eunuchs who have been made eunuchs by others—and there are those who choose to live like eunuchs for the sake of the kingdom of heaven. The one who can accept this should accept it."

Observation/Interpretation:
Jesus laid down a pretty hard standard. He raised the value of women to be equal to men. More than that, He went back beyond Deuteronomy all the way to Genesis to remind everyone that the couple no longer functions as two people, but rather one person.

When the disciples threw up their hands in exasperation saying, "it is better not to marry," they were not unlike many who will read this book. They felt like marriage would be impossible, so why even try? Jesus didn't pull back on His verbal barbs. It might be wise for them to be single. Those who could not accept a woman as an equal in a marriage would have to renounce marriage so that they could lift up the kingdom.

APPLICATION

- You are equal in value to the person you marry.

- You must evaluate whether or not you can accept Christ's standard for marriage before you marry.

- You must enter marriage believing only death will separate you.

chapter three:
SINGLENESS & MARRIAGE

Singleness

"What if I have the gift of singleness?" Terror erupts from single people as this realization sweeps over them. This might be the most emotionally driven statement that causes panic in young men and women. They might as well have said, "What if I have stage IV cancer?" Let me ease some of the dramatics with a simple statement. If God has called you to be single, you will know it. If you are terrified of doing something that is not in your born-again- nature to do, then God probably isn't calling you to it.

The gift of singleness isn't like being conscripted to do something you absolutely hate. Missionaries in Africa don't sit around whining about how God called them to Africa. They love Africa. They love the African people. They aren't too worried about missing out on the latest fad of American culture. The same is true for the gift of singleness. I have a cousin-in-law, Jennifer, that is single and is quite content. She doesn't sit around pining for men.

I even had her write an appendix to those who are single and terrified so they would realize singleness is not in their DNA. Some singles are so unbelievably terrified they might be forever single that they make relationships an idol.

See Appendix: Singleness for Jennifer's real life illustration on wanting singleness

When called to do something, you *want* to do it. God laid it on your heart. For those who accept the calling of singleness, there is a relief they no longer have to look for a spouse. Married life doesn't hold the same appeal for them as it does the typical single.

I know a lot of you aren't convinced by this, but let's see what scripture says. Paul, the advocate for the gift of singleness, had a lot to say about marriage and confirmed bachelorhood. Let's hone in on what he actually said and make clear what he didn't say. The main passage that Paul speaks on when it comes to the married life versus the single life is 1 Corinthians 7.

Before we go on, we must make one thing clear. There were two kinds of people in Corinth: the super-prude and the super-promiscuous. The super-prude thought any sensual indulgence was evil, and the super-promiscuous were having sex with their dad's wife. Paul had really hammered the sensual people in chapters two through six. He turned his attention to the super-prude in chapter seven. There were some who thought that a married man shouldn't have sex with his wife. Paul took aim at that.

The Corinthians had such division over these issues that they wrote Paul a letter asking him to clarify what exactly was right and what wasn't. Paul, in this section of his letter, responded to their question. He first quoted the statement back to them from their letter written to Paul.

1 Corinthians 7:1 (NIV)
    Now for the matters you wrote about: It is good for a man
    not to marry.

I grew up on the NIV. For the most part, it's pretty trust worthy, but here I think the translators botched it. Let's look at how the other well-known translations handle this verse.

1 Corinthians 7:1			
NASV	NLT	ESV	NIV
Now concerning the things about which you wrote, it is good for a man **not to touch a woman.**	Now regarding the questions you asked in your letter. Yes, it is good to **live a celibate life.**	Now concerning the matters about which you wrote: "It is good for a man **not to have sexual relations with a woman.**	Now for the matters you wrote about: It is good for a man **not to marry.**

Here is a literal translation of the Greek.

1 Corinthians 7:1a	
Περὶ	concerning, about, around
δὲ	but, now
ἐγράψατε	you all wrote

A direct translation of this phrase:

"Now, about what you wrote,"

Paul set this up to directly answer questions that the Corinthians had sent Paul in their own letter. Paul quoted back to them their question in the following phrase:

1 Corinthians 7:1b	
καλὸν	good
ἀνθρώπῳ	man
γυναικὸς	wife, woman—it's used for both
μὴ	no
ἅπτεσθαι	to touch

A direct translation of this phrase is:

"It is good for man (men in general) not to touch a woman (or a wife)."

Paul tackled a common saying that contained a euphemism. So it would look like this, "It's good for a man (married or unmarried) not to have sex with any woman (including his wife).

This puts a whole new spin on the phrase, doesn't it? The Corinthians wanted to know Paul's take on a common slogan known to the Christian Corinthians and with which Paul was equally familiar.

Look how this works in context with the next verse. Every version says essentially the same thing.

1 Corinthians 7:2 (ESV)
> But because of the temptation to sexual immorality, each man should have his own wife and each woman her own husband.

Paul wasn't being asked if it was better for a man not to marry. He was being asked if men (married or unmarried) should not have sex. Paul's response then makes sense. He said, "Yeah that's a good saying for unmarried men, but let me correct it for the married dudes."

A married man must have sex with his wife. A married woman must have sex with her husband. Otherwise, there might be a temptation to look for that elsewhere. Even high school students know that once the sexual Pandora's box has been opened, only an act of God can close it again.

Verses 2-6 clarify Paul's message to the married. Verses 7-9 clarify for the unmarried.

1 Corinthians 7:7-9 (NET)
> I wish that everyone was as I am. But each has his own gift from God, one this way, another that. To the unmarried and widows I say that it is best for them to remain as I am. But if they do not have self-control, let them get married. For it is better to marry than to burn with sexual desire.

Observation/Interpretation:
Paul just got plain practical. He said that it's better to marry than to have these urges which might cause you to sin.

APPLICATION

- You should get married before your desires cause you to sin.

Marriage doesn't free you from lust, but it sure doesn't hurt. It also takes care of that *needing* to find a relationship issue. Sex on a consistent basis is satisfying. You don't *need* sex. It's not a use it or lose it principle. Appendages don't start falling off due to lack of use.

Here is the weird part. I'm not begging my wife for sex. Sex isn't the ultimate thing like I once thought it was. I had made sex this demi-god. I thought once I got it, I would reach a new level of joy. But it's not. It's an important part of marriage, but it isn't even close to the most important thing. For a guy, I compare it to having ESPN SportsCenter. You love SportsCenter. You watch SportsCenter whenever it comes on, but you don't think about it all day long. If you took a vacation, you could go a week without it (if you're healthy).

I know that sounds ridiculous. I know it does. When you are unmarried and some of you men are masturbating sometimes twice a night and the thought that you won't crave sex like a wild man once you are married seems absurd.

Since we are being honest here, let me address what I know some of you are doing. You are having sex or pushing the limits physically because you know you are going to get married anyway. I'm not sure how to delicately put this, so I'll just shoot you straight. You are heading for disaster. The only reason that what you are doing physically now is so stimulating is because you know you shouldn't be doing it. Right? I mean c'mon.

Here is the reality. You and your boyfriend want to please God. You try to keep your hands off each other—until it gets to be 2am. Then your mind goes on vacation, and you end up "going too far." Once you have gone that far, you create a new boundary. You convince yourself that you're doing great, because at least you didn't go all the way.

Let me break it down for you. Get married or break up. Men,

if you are not ready to get married, you are still a boy and need to break up. There is no condemnation here. If you are not ready to provide for a wife, then you shouldn't be enjoying what God created solely for marriage. A price will be paid. It's only a matter of time before you reap what you have sown. If you are ready, then you need to throw down a proposal.

I know this is harsh, but if she is hot enough to touch sensually, then she is hot enough to marry. If she is non-psycho enough to touch sensually, then she is non-psycho enough to marry. If she is mature enough to touch sensually, she is mature enough to marry. Am I getting through here? Your excuses about how messed up your girlfriend is—are lame. If you are able to date her and not cross the boundaries physically, then continue on figuring out one another. Once you cross the physical line, you find yourself in a weird dilemma which will make you date for five years, because you are never sure.

Ladies, you really only get one choice on this one when you cross physical boundaries. You could pull a Ruth (we'll discuss that in a later chapter), or you can break off the relationship.

Some of you are going to say, "What if we only messed up once? Do we need to break it off?" Ask the Holy Spirit on that one. Get other believers involved. I just find it strange that you can share the most intimate things with one another emotionally and physically, then be like, "I don't know if I can marry her."

Remember, I get it. I did the same thing you did for years. I paid the price. It's not worth it. Unrepentant impurity is a never-ending cycle that produces nothing but heartache.

I'm going to pause on the exegesis for a moment to camp in this awkward spot. Some of you have made bold statements that you would die for Christ—even if that meant some remote mission field. Some of you have done some crazy bold stuff for Jesus, but on this particular issue, you have the spiritual stamina of wet bread.

My ministry was hindered for years, because I dabbled in the in-between. I could lead men in combat, but I struggled for so long with purity. I did the same things you do and justified pushing boundaries, because I really felt that I would get married. Several relationships later, I actually did.

I wonder what would have happened if I had grown up sooner. How much further my ministry might have extended? How many friendships would still be in tact if I had been able to boldly make the decision to live for Christ—not just die for Him. God is sovereign, and whatever I intended for evil, God can use for good. I believe that. God is in the redemption business. He can make beauty from ashes. I want you to believe that. I also want you to grow up and be a man—or a woman.

Marriage

Paul then moved to the married folks and directly addressed them.

1 Corinthians 7:10-11 (ESV)

To the married I give this command (not I, but the Lord): A wife must not separate from her husband. But if she does, she must remain unmarried or else be reconciled to her husband. And a husband must not divorce his wife.

Observation/Interpretation

Paul answered directly the question about that particular saying about men not touching women sensually through verse 16.

Paul transitioned to the main point. Don't worry about who to marry. He wanted them to get ready for the Lord to return. They should stay in whatever situation God called them and not look to change it. Paul wanted a divorced person to either remarry their former spouse or stay unmarried. Initially divorced people read that and their body aches, because they feel stuck. We will get deeper into what happens if you are divorced in Chapter 19.

The point Paul pushed here was stay where God called you. He continued that thought all the way through verse 24. I think that the most powerful verse in chapter seven is verse 21.

1 Corinthians 7:21 (NET)

Were you called as a slave? Do not worry about it. But if indeed you are able to be free, make the most of the opportunity.

Observation/Interpretation:

Paul wanted the Corinthians to focus on heaven. He wanted their focus on Christ and not on gaining freedom. He then brought common sense into the picture so that believers didn't just live a fatalistic life and not accept advancement in any way for the Lord. That is on the realm of ridiculous and Paul knew that and gave the go ahead to freedom. If Paul gave the go ahead on freedom from slavery, the same conclusion can be drawn for marriage.

APPLICATION

- You should not be so focused on getting married that you lose your focus for the Lord.

- You have the freedom to marry or not to marry.

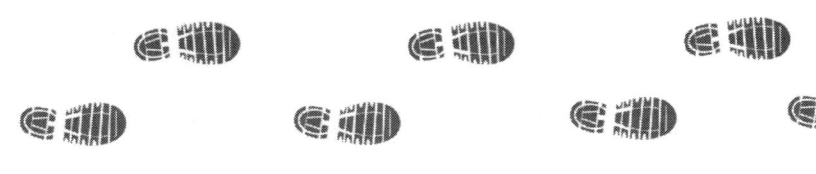

What if I'm single, but not called to be?

I know there are some of you are not called to be single, but are. You have friends that are working on child number three and you are scanning Facebook for new prospects. I'm not going to say this goes for everyone, but the problem could be you. It may be that you are looking for marriage to make you happy. I'm not talking sex here, I'm talking about looking for a spouse to serve us, rather than to serve.

How many times have you heard someone say, "I just want a wife to help me in my ministry." Many view this as noble because it deals with ministry, but it still focuses on what the guy wants. Have you heard someone say, "I just want a wife that I can serve and meet her needs."

Do you see the difference? The media doesn't sell marriage that way, but that is the reality. In the book, *Sacred Marriage*, Gary Thomas asked, "What if God designed marriage to make us holy more than to make us happy?" When people read that, they slapped their foreheads and sighed. Of course, God designed marriage to make us holy and not happy. That doesn't mean that God doesn't want us to be happy. That means happiness cannot be our ultimate goal. Being like Christ is our ultimate goal.

Jesus got on his knees and washed his discples feet. The Son of God served those He loved. So what if singles turned the question around and stopped asking, "What person can serve my needs best?" and started asking, "What person would I like to serve for the rest of my life?" That change in question might change the rest of your life. Think of the implications that might have on who you find attractive. Does that change the type of person you are interested in if you ask yourself of who you want to serve the rest of your life?

Paul got around to talking about those who were unmarried but wanted to be. Like many Americans, they didn't feel the call to be single.

1 Corinthians 7:25-28 (NIV)
> Now about virgins: I have no command from the Lord,
> but I give a judgment as one who by the Lord's mercy is

trustworthy. Because of the present crisis, I think that it
is good for a man to remain as he is. Are you pledged to a
woman? Do not seek to be released. Are you free from such a
commitment? Do not look for a wife.

But if you do marry, you have not sinned; and if a virgin
marries, she has not sinned. But those who marry will face
many troubles in this life, and I want to spare you this.

Observation/Interpretation:

What is the "present crisis?" It was probably a combination of
things. The Corinthian church was a mess with what was going on
among its members. Paul also lived like Jesus was coming back immi-
nently—as we have somehow forgotten to live. Paul lived in the last
days. This would be the time when Jesus returned. We know that
from what Jesus said about his return and what Paul wrote about in
his letters to the Thessalonians that the last days would be difficult.
If he had a family to support, he would have left them widowed and
orphaned when he was decapitated for his faith in Rome.

Although we too are in the last days, the Western culture has not
seen near the persecution that the early church has or those who are
believers today in the Middle East or in South East Asia. I think that
brings it into a more clear perspective for us. If a virgin was about to
be chased, imprisoned, or killed for her faith, that might not be the
best time to start a family.

That is what Paul had to face and he wanted to spare them this
trouble. He didn't want to spare them marital trouble—like getting into arguments. That is what sanctifies us. Trust me, I am a
far better Christian now that I am married than when I was single.
Marriage forces you to look at yourself in the mirror and grow up.
You can't simply remain immature when someone gets to see your
stuff every day.

Paul further explained what he meant about wanting to spare the
married troubles in this life, because of the tribulations they face.
I have heard this verse quoted by preachers for an easy laugh. They
would quote, "But those who marry will face many troubles in this
life, and I want to spare you this." They joke that Paul knew how
tough marriage would be, and that is why he stayed single.

That joke is still so over used that I started to believe it. It has been told so many times, people now assume that Paul didn't want to hassle with date night.

Paul wanted to spare men and women from raising a family in such a harsh environment. He further explained this in verses 29-35.

1 Corinthians 7:29-35 (NIV2010)

What I mean, brothers and sisters, is that the time is short. From now on those who have wives should live as if they do not; those who mourn, as if they did not; those who are happy, as if they were not; those who buy something, as if it were not theirs to keep; those who use the things of the world, as if not engrossed in them. For this world in its present form is passing away. I would like you to be free from concern.

An unmarried man is concerned about the Lord's affairs—how he can please the Lord. But a married man is concerned about the affairs of this world—how he can please his wife—and his interests are divided. An unmarried woman or virgin is concerned about the Lord's affairs: Her aim is to be devoted to the Lord in both body and spirit.

But a married woman is concerned about the affairs of this world—how she can please her husband. I am saying this for your own good, not to restrict you, but that you may live in a right way in undivided devotion to the Lord.

Observation/Interpretation:

Paul encouraged his readers to use their singleness for the purpose of the Lord. He held the opinion that one could serve God more if he was single, than if he was married. Getting arrested, traveling all over the Roman world, and never having a stable income are just about as anti-family as one can imagine. Even today with all of the superior modes of transportation and comforts, it is difficult for a family to be on the road and doing ministry. Add to that, persecution and no mini-van, problems start to rise up for the minister and his family.

Paul didn't guilt trip anyone about getting married. Those who married during those difficult times were clearly not sinning.

1 Corinthians 7:36- 37 (NIV)
> If anyone thinks he is acting improperly toward the virgin he is engaged to, and if she is getting along in years and he feels he ought to marry, he should do as he wants. He is not sinning. They should get married.
>
> But the man who has settled the matter in his own mind, who is under no compulsion but has control over his own will, and who has made up his mind not to marry the virgin—this man also does the right thing.

Observation/Interpretation:
Paul clarified the sinless position of those who wanted to get married. He concluded his thoughts on virgins marrying by saying another thing that without context can be very confusing.

1 Corinthians 7:38 (NIV)
> So then, he who marries the virgin does right, but he who does not marry her does better.

Observation/Interpretation:
I know I have repeated this, but this verse has caused several young people to freak out and wonder if they are really supposed to be single. Paul wanted those facing persecution to have a one-focused mind. Serve the Lord. Jesus doesn't even know the hour of His return. Paul didn't know when Jesus would return. We don't know when Jesus will return, but we ought to live as though He may at any time. Because of the freedoms that the U.S. still has, we don't have to worry about the same persecution that Christians in the early church or Christians in danger today have around the world.

For a Christian today to live like he is in the last days might mean that he live a life devoted to the Lord by moving his family to the inner city, then have everyone do street ministry. It might mean being married or unmarried and moving to a third world country and giving everythinghe has so that a national of the country you move to might get the gospel. However, it also might mean raising up a family in the Lord, sharing the gospel with friends and always seeking to expand his circle of influence.

1 Corinthians 7:39-40

> A woman is bound to her husband as long as he lives. But if her husband dies, she is free to marry anyone she wishes, but he must belong to the Lord. In my judgment, she is happier if she stays as she is—and I think that I too have the Spirit of God.

Observation/Interpretation:

Paul then explained how long married people are bound to each other—until death. Paul transitioned to an observation that I don't completely understand. He made a case for her happiness in that she won't have invested herself into a husband who might be hunted down and killed for believing the crazy notion that Jesus died and rose again.

Interestingly enough here was the rare occasion that Paul wanted the person to choose whatever felt best. It seems anti-Christian, doesn't it? In our Christian piety we have been taught that we must live our lives based on obedience and not on feeling. How many times has some good intentioned person said something absolutely moronic, "Once you stop looking, then God will bring that special person to you."

I cringe when I think how many times that sort of weight has been put on someone. It's like you have to trick yourself into feeling like you don't want to be married. We don't do this with anything else. Even the most self-righteous Christians don't sit on the couch and say, "I'm just praying that the Lord will bring me food to eat." Or "I'm just praying that the Lord sends a check so I can make it month to month." No, you get off the couch and go to Wal-Mart and get some food or get a job.

Paul wanted the woman to choose singleness based on her ability to be happy. Granted the word for *happy* here is also *blessed*. So you could read it, "In my judgment, she is more blessed if she stays as she is..." but it is a judgment call by Paul and not a conditional response based on her choice.

APPLICATION

- If you feel you would be happier or blessed being married—do it.

- If you feel that you would be happier or more blessed being single—do it.

In my opinion you will be happier if you are married and I think that I too have the Spirit of God.

Don't fear the "gift" of singleness. If you have it, you will know it, and you will want it. In all probability if you are dreading singleness like contracting a fatal disease, then you probably don't have it. God is not calling you to it. That doesn't mean if you are called to singleness there won't be periods of loneliness, just like for married people, there are seasons of "Did I marry Darth Vader?" I'm not preaching prosperity gospel here, so don't hear me wrong. Just understand that God allows you to be happy.

In fact, God rejoices over your marriage and is excited about your sex life. Just read Song of Solomon. For single people feeling terrified, you may have to cling to Psalm 37:4. Trust in your Heavenly Father and enjoy Him and then ultimately you will have the desires of your heart. That may not be a spouse, but we must come to the place where we understand He is a good Father and a good Father won't subject you to a life of misery.

chapter four:
CHRISTIAN SUBMISSION

If you are still convinced that you want to get married, then let's continue on to what relationships look like with a husband and a wife. Ephesians 5:22-33 is a fantastic place to start. Paul did a masterful job of describing a man's relationship to his wife and a woman's relationship to her husband, while at the same time speaking of the mystery of Christ and the church. Earlier in Ephesians 5, Paul listed out how we are to live:

➢ Be imitators of God.

➢ Live like Christ.

➢ Don't participate in sexual immorality.

➢ Don't joke about sexual immorality.

> ➤ Don't be involved in any immorality.

> ➤ Bring darkness to light and seek to be like Christ.

> ➤ Be filled with the Spirit.

> > ❖ Address one another with awesome songs.

> > ❖ Give thanks to God.

> > ❖ Submit to one another out of the fear of the Lord.

Paul listed out how we all are to live. Then he turned the corner and wrote further about being filled with the Spirit. Having uplifting conversations with one another and giving thanks to God didn't require much explanation. Submission did. Amazing how nothing has changed in 2,000 years.

Paul brought to light three different relationships which showed submission and a fear of the Lord: wives and husbands, parents and children, and slaves and masters. The latter two are in chapter 6 which we always assumed was the armor of God chapter. We skipped over verses 1-9 to get to the good stuff. Admit it. You've done that. Especially about slaves, because you didn't think that it applied. Some of you might as well be slaves chained to a cubicle working 70-80 hour weeks.

These are clear relationships where submission to the one person is like submission to the Lord. The welfare of the submitter is then put into the hands of the one that is in control, much like the Lord who is ultimately in control of our lives. Some people try to say that the word *submit* doesn't really mean submit.

The word *submit* comes from the Greek word 'υποτασσόμενοι, which means to subject oneself to another. It was a military term meaning to voluntarily subject oneself to another. That is what happens in the military. When you sign up, you learn how to be a whole new person by subjecting yourself to the system and the people of that structure.

In Greek, you can borrow a verb from the previous sentence and infer it into the following sentence. We do it in English sometimes, but here is how it looks word-for-word.

Verse 21 Ὑποτασσόμενοι ἀλλήλοις ἐν φόβῳ Χριστοῦ	
Ὑποτασσόμενοι	submitting to
ἀλλήλοις	one another
ἐν	In
φόβῳ	fear/reverence
Χριστοῦ	to Christ

Verse 22 αἱ γυναῖκες τοῖς ἰδίοις ἀνδράσιν ὡς τῷ κυρίῳ	
αἱ	The
γυναῖκες	Wives
τοῖς	The
ἰδίοις	one's own
ἀνδράσιν	Husband
ὡς	As
τῷ	The
κυρίῳ	Lord

Observation/Interpretation:

A lot of us grew up reading a Bible that divided verse 21 from verse 22. But in reality, they aren't. Verse 21 sets up the submission piece as how to live in the Spirit. Verse 22 says, "wives (obey) your own husband as to the Lord." What a difficult thing to grasp! We see Paul isn't just having wives obey husbands as to the Lord, but children obeying parents and slaves obeying masters. Think of obeying your boss like he was Jesus.

You're given three relational opportunities to practice living in the Spirit: with your spouse, with your parents/kids, and with your boss/subordinates.

Most everyone will deal with these three relationships. Wives, children, and slaves were to obey their respective God-ordained leader as obeying Jesus himself. The thought of obeying anyone other than Jesus, like he were Jesus, is kind of ridiculous. That shows faith.

To put faith in Christ—to obey a person who may mistreat you—is evidence of faith lived out. A reliance on the Lord is being truly expressed. When we look out for our own welfare, the Lord is taken out of the picture.

In verses 22-24, Paul spoke to the wives.

Ephesians 5:22-24 (ESV)
    Wives, submit to your own husbands, as to the Lord. For the husband is the head of the wife even as Christ is the head of the church, his body, and is himself its Savior. Now as the church submits to Christ, so also wives should submit in everything to their husbands.

Observation/Interpretation:
    Not much wiggle room here for those that want to take "obey" out of their vows. These verses make a lot of women nervous, but these verses should make men nervous. Think about how much responsibility a man has to lead his wife well. Her role is to submit to his authority and be his helpmate. The success and failure of this dance is all on the man. She follows his lead.
    Many scholars have argued that Paul here doesn't really mean "everything." They note that in Acts 5, Sapphiara should not have sinned with her husband Annanais, and her death proved that. However, when we start to say that wives should only obey their husbands when they are godly, how will they ever know when they are to obey? You might as well command women to obey their husbands, except when they are PMSing, because, well, no woman can be held accountable for that.
    What if a woman marries an abusive husband that beats his wife to a pulp? In the US alone, this happens a lot. The woman marries a man and then finds herself a victim. Many times the man's issues could have been seen before marriage, but the emotion swept them away and then the wife wakes up one day with a black eye and pounding headache wondering who exactly it was that she married.
    The hypothetical lists that can be created are endless. For many women, they aren't hypothetical. Every now and then, a husband

gets beat by his wife. No, I'm not kidding. I've counseled that couple as well. So how do we handle it when a woman is getting persecuted by her own husband? How do we handle it when her husband is sinning against her? The Bible actually does get into this.

In Matthew 5, the beatitudes describe how the woman is to react to her enemy. Matthew 18 describes how to handle a believer who is sinning against another believer. The community of believers, the church, is that woman's protector in the case of an abusive relationship. That is why it is so important for couples to live in community.

If a husband sins against the wife, she brings his sin to him. If he repents, then she forgives him. If he doesn't repent, then she brings in one or two others from her church. If he still doesn't repent, she takes him before the church. And if he still doesn't repent, then he is treated like an unbeliever. The husband and wife stay separated until the church sees genuine repentance. That is how it is handled.

I only went into that because sometimes people are so worried about draconian men who are going to use the Bible to get the woman to submit. The great thing about the Bible calling the wife to submit is that the same Bible can be used for the man to submit to his pastor, separating him from his wife for a while he learns to treat his wife appropriately.

Paul wasn't naïve when he wrote this. He had scripture before him. The process for handling sin wasn't vague because people lived in community. The mega-church wasn't around quite yet. Don't get me wrong. I love the mega-church and am a member of one. When you go to church to hear a sermon, but don't get involved in a smaller group of people who know your dirty laundry, then what you have is a rock concert with an uplifting message. That isn't church. I know that might rub people the wrong way. We all agree that the church isn't a building, so let's settle the issue that church isn't a worship service.

Notice that Paul didn't give her anything else to do and limits his challenge to the woman to do one thing: submit like the church submits to Jesus.

Paul turned his attention to husbands in verses 25-30.

Ephesians 5:25-30 (ESV)

Husbands, love your wives, as Christ loved the church and gave himself up for her, that he might sanctify her, having cleansed her by the washing of water with the word, so that he might present the church to himself in splendor, without spot or wrinkle or any such thing, that she might be holy and without blemish.

In the same way husbands should love their wives as their own bodies. He who loves his wife loves himself. For no one ever hated his own flesh, but nourishes and cherishes it, just as Christ does the church, because we are members of his body.

Therefore a man shall leave his father and mother and hold fast to his wife, and the two shall become one flesh."

This mystery is profound, and I am saying that it refers to Christ and the church. However, let each one of you love his wife as himself, and let the wife see that she respects her husband.

Observation/Interpretation:

Paul gave the man one obligation. Love your wife like she is you. Whenever I do weddings, I quote this verse and then tell the groom, "From now on when you see your wife, I no longer want you to say, 'I love you,' but rather say, 'I love me.'"

This is the ideal world. For someone in the dating realm, you can see if the person you are dating shows any signs of these principles. If a woman is able to obey her father as if the Lord, you can almost be guaranteed she will obey her husband. She has been trained right. If she is rebellious towards her father, she is going to be rebellious towards her husband.

I know there are a billion different excuses, like what if her father is abusive or a drunk or something where she has to disobey him? There are always exceptions, but watch the woman. If she obeys authority, she won't have a problem obeying her husband. If she is always seeking to find a way to rebel, then she will rebel against her husband.

Same goes for men. Watch how he follows the golden rule. If he loves the Lord with all his heart, soul, mind, and strength, then he is a keeper, because he will be treating his neighbor as himself, even if his neighbor is a Samaritan. See Luke 10 for that reference. But let's not kid ourselves. A guy that good is usually already taken. So is the woman who isn't rebellious. They tend to get snatched up pretty quick.

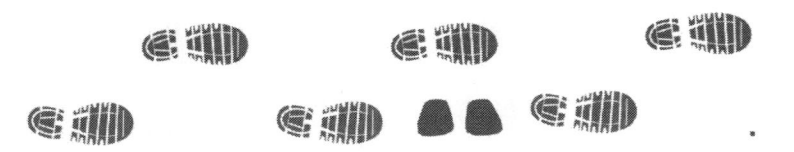

section three

THE WAY THINGS ARE

War is messy. As a combat veteran I can tell you that although warfare has been waged for as long as men have existed on the planet, we still haven't mastered it. The enemy always gets a vote.

The fog of war is a term used to describe the lack of communication, the isolation, and the relative chaos of the battlefield. I never expected to have car bombs explode and sheer off an arm of one of my men, but it happened. I never expected to lose my first soldier in the first four minutes of combat, but that happened, too. My men had to deal with that. I had to deal with that. That is war.

However, over time my men and I developed strategies to deal with the chaos. We were able to see the enemy's tactics and defeat them before he was able to detonate the bomb, fire his sniper rifle, or launch an RPG. It just took some training and for us to learn from our mistakes. We also had to discipline ourselves not to become complacent.

The fog of dating can be chaotic.

Several years ago I took my girlfriend to the New York Supper Club. It would be our time to shine and have an exceedingly good time. I loved it. She was dressed to the nines' in an elegant black dress, and I was in a suit and tie.

We strode out onto the dance floor and for a moment, it was blissful. Everyone stopped what they were doing to watch us as my date spun and spun. In my excitement of an audience, I wanted to try some new things. I wanted to explore our dancing and just let the rhythm take us away.

The hard part was this. I was a completely mechanical dancer. I didn't have rhythm. I danced to the beat of my own drum. I could get away with it when I was spinning my partner and doing difficult maneuvers, but when it came back to a time of giving her a break and going through a simple dance step, I flopped.

I was terrible. In the grand scheme of things, who cares? I did. I not only walked off the dance floor in frustration, but I blamed her for her inability to follow. I stormed off the dance floor and gave her a tongue lashing for her inability to follow.

I then translated it to our relationship. She cried, and I was furious. Looking back I still feel sorry for her and the horrific journey I took her on. I had broken all my own rules of dance (which I hadn't made up yet).

I wanted to do the difficult dance moves before I mastered the simple moves. In sports, athletes get this. Athletes will spend hours upon hours studying the basics of a lay-up, or spend hours in a batting cage, or hours at the driving range. Athletes will spend hours mastering the basic steps to the foundation of the game. Then, when they play, it looks effortless.

I didn't have a dance coach. I just jumped in and started dancing. That is great, until you think you are better than you are. That was my problem. I had become God's gift to dancing, and I was the only one who knew it. I made countless partners pay the price of my pride.

Rhythm was something that I had to learn over time. It took me forever to just feel the music and go with it. When trying to "Two

Step," I resembled more of the "Robot."

Eventually, after a ton of coaching, I got to the place where I didn't have to think about dancing.

The music swept me away. I didn't look at my partner's feet, and I didn't worry about the steps. I just danced. However, it took people pointing out what I was doing wrong. I'd always assumed I was doing it right, and my partner was the one who wasn't following me.

I always find it funny that we expect people to automatically know how to interact with the opposite sex. After sin entered the world, man was left looking pretty desperate. Sin ruined the dance that God created for us to enjoy. So a relationship that we once thought was wonderful and perfect became so out of rhythm, it was unrecognizable.

Christ rescued us from our off-beat rhythm and redeemed us to perfection. Yet, for most of us, we don't feel perfect.

We haven't been trained. We haven't had lessons. Our cluelessness has resulted in chaos.

Most have experienced improvement for a season. When patience wears thin, we find ourselves in the same chaos we experienced before our rescue.

In this section, I want to reveal some of the blunders that you have already experienced. Some are funny when read, but tragic when lived.

chapter five: BROKEN MARRIAGES

Most singles in their twenties and thirties are terrified of marrying the *wrong one*. Looking at the carnage of divorce and blended families, some have just checked out completely on the broken institution.

Divorce Rates
41% of first time marriages end in divorce
60% of second marriages end in divorce
74% of third marriages end in divorce.

Let me give you a breakdown of the disaster. A study by Barna Research group reveals that 25% of all adults have been divorced at least once in their life. No wonder young adults stiff-arm the idea of marriage. I guess it should come as no surprise then that the highest number of divorces occur in men and women 20-25 years old. These numbers don't include the vast amount of couples who live together, have children, and aren't married. The stability factor is gone.

63% of kids grow up with both biological parents. That means that almost 40% of children grow up seeing the example of their parents walking out to solve their differences.

As per the National Center for Health Statistics (NCHS), 25% of marriage within younger couples is 'predicted' to end within 10 years, and the rates increase to 43% in 15 years.

Women with kids initiate around 70% of divorce cases.

Divorce Reasons in America

Stats are just stats without reasons and without people. I get that. I don't want to spend too many pages of this book reading the woes of marriage. I'm not here to scare you out of it. I just wanted to take a brief look at why things are the way they are. I'm not sure if all these are really the reasons they got divorced. It's just what people have said were the reasons.

> ➤ Cohabitation. 85% of couples who decide to get married after cohabitation end up getting divorce. So much for the test drive.

> ➤ Lack of communication. In the marriage there was the feeling of mutual non-understanding. The couple expressed feeling the ball and chain of marriage and having no freedom. Common words to describe this are as follows: misunderstandings, arguments, frustrations and failed expectations.

> ➤ 66% of divorced couples are childless. That isn't the cause necessarily, but it is a reason why the marriage doesn't last.

Some reasons don't need an explanation.

> ➢ Money
>
> ➢ Infidelity
>
> ➢ Abusive behavior
>
> ➢ Sexual incompatibility
>
> ➢ Addiction

See Appendix: Broken Marriage for a real life illustration

chapter six:
COHABITATION

Because of the divorce rate, many feel the need to conduct a test drive. After all, you wouldn't buy a car without taking her for a spin first, would you?

Here is a recent Facebook message I received.

Subject: Is it wrong to live together and not be married?

I need some help. Do you have any sermons or discussions on marriage and the Bible? What is the Bible's description of marriage? Can you be "married" in God's eyes, but not be legally married? I don't think God's idea of being married meant you have to file taxes together, buy a home together and share each other's debt!

If two people are committed to one another and intend on

spending their lives together, then wouldn't that be considered "married" in the eyes of God? Does someone have to sign a piece of paper and file taxes together for God to consider them married?

This woman didn't see "oneness" as her ultimate goal for marriage. She liked the companionship part of things. She liked the sexual part of things. However, financially she liked to be completely independent. As her boyfriend goes down financially, she suffers no consequences, other than the fact that she has a freeloader who doesn't pull his weight living with her.

No, cohabitation is not biblical oneness. It's way-outness. It doesn't honor God. Don't try to pull the, "We're just gonna live together and not have sex," line. Stop lying to yourself.

But if you don't believe me for biblical reasons, here are some realities about couples who cohabitate prior to marriage.

Houston Chronicle reported that those who live together have an 80% greater chance of getting a divorce than those that don't.

A Washington State researcher reported women who cohabitate are twice as likely to experience domestic violence than married women.

71% of the women out of 100 couples said they would never cohabitate again.

chapter seven:
FACING DATING REALITIES

Carnal Christian Singles

Your church hasn't been the bastion of purity. The exhortation for being godly from your overweight youth pastor with the spiky hair and ratty Chuck Taylors fell on deaf ears. In college and as a young adult, church has seemed like more of a cattle call than it has a place to seek out a wife or husband.

Christians are becoming more like the world in terms of their sexuality. The media bombards us with images, thoughts, and perverted acts. Our sensibilities have been rocked to a point that we have no boundaries. Our sin nature, which we know to be wicked, is the very thing we feed when sleeping with our significant other is reduced to a "no big deal" type thing, where friends aren't real friends if they don't let it slide.

Fish Bowl

The fish bowl exists whether you want to acknowledge it or not. A fishbowl is any environment where you know everyone and you get updates on the lives of people you never talk to faster than news-feeds on Facebook or Twitter. The fishbowl gets a bad rap, but it isn't all bad. There is real community in the fishbowl.

However, with real community comes real gossip. With real gossip comes real hurt and pain. But the same mechanism that has caused so much pain can also be helpful in preventing it.

God didn't design humans to long for community so they would end up hating each other or relentlessly compete with one another destroying friendships. That was never the plan. Sin has a way of marring that which God made perfect.

See Appendix: Fish Bowl for a real life illustration

Silver Bullet

You get one shot. One girl or one guy. One relationship to figure out marriage. Once it doesn't go well, the person you dated is off limits to everyone you know. It's kind of like marked territory. One attempt at a relationship and then you will be forever etched in the minds of those on the dating scene as being off limits.

See Appendix: Silver Bullet for a real life illustration

Secret Dating

Because of the fishbowl's anti-grace tendencies and silver bullet labeling, there is a tendency to become secret daters. Secret dating is hanging out with a "friend" in ways that only those who are dating would spend time together, but calling it, "just friends." That prevents people from asking too many questions and getting accused of shooting your silver bullet. Secret dating happens many times when potential couples cross boundaries and don't want to be castigated for their sins.

See Appendix: Secret Dating for a real life illustration

Emotional Dumping

The act of sharing all of one's intimate information all at once with a stranger.

This usually happens in public. It usually happens when no one is expecting it to happen, and these are the words that you hear repeated over and over again.

"I just can't believe how connected we are and we just met!"

Emotional dumping, more times than not leads to the pains of secret dating.

See Appendix: Emotional Dumping for a real life illustration

chapter eight:
DATING TYPES
TO AVOID

The Creeper

She has the stroller that she keeps in the trunk because she knows "it" will happen one day soon.

He is socially awkward and doesn't know it. He is very overt in his appeal for your love, and you don't know what to do with him.

Online Super-Hero

He friended every girl on your Facebook and has sent them an awkward message, "Hey, I saw you on Bill's page and thought I'd say 'Hi.'"

He's been on every dating website, gone to every single event, and seriously considered a mail order bride.

Sex-user

This looks like a three-year-relationship, and he stayed with her just for sex. She thinks that he will eventually come around, and maybe he will. This is a painfully long dating relationship that causes heartache long after a miracle "I do" is said.

Battered Wife Syndrome

While several of these are humorous, this one is not. The guy gets emotional control over the girl because the emotional insecurity was too strong for both. He has to have a weak woman who will take his abuse, and she needs someone to control her. The warped sense of right leads her to say things like, "I always pick the losers." For abusive men, they usually label their girlfriends as "psycho."

No Self Esteem

This is the guy who is decent, but he doesn't believe it. He feels more comfortable around the "least of these" than he does with regular folks. People who are projects don't reject like those who can hold their own.

He is likely to marry the woman who got divorced yesterday and has three kids and is 24. He considers himself a thinker and on any given day would give you the shirt off his back. He never asks for help because in his mind there are other more serious issues going on.

This can go for the woman as well. She justs wants someone to love her, and if she pulls him out of the pit, he will "owe" her.

This goes bad because most people don't view themselves as projects, or if they do, once they get on their feet, they move on leaving the person with no self esteem worse off than when they began.

Missionary Dater

I had a roommate once say, "It's easier to make a hot girl a Christian than it is to make a Christian hot."

The problem is your definition of hot is cleavage and flesh. Christ's definition of hot is how in love with Him she is.

For women, they have been around non-committal Christians for so long they are relieved to find men interested and willing to give a relationship a shot. In their minds, they get the feeling that they can make this work one day.

It sometimes works. Sometimes guys grab hold of the gospel based on the inspiration from their girlfriend. It happens. I won't lie and say it doesn't.

People also win the lottery. Blind squirrels find nuts. Broken clocks are right twice a day.

See Appendix: Missionary Dater for a real life illustration

Voice of God Dater

I'm sure you have had this happen to you at one time or another. The creepy guy walks up out of nowhere and says, "God told me that we are supposed to be together."

Or the girl that you have been dating for a while comes out of nowhere with, "God told me we are supposed to be married."

The problem with God telling one person something this dramatic but not revealing it to the other leads me to view the "Voice of God Dating" technique to be one of total manipulation.

For those of you who do hear the voice of God on occasion, how has that worked for you? If the person got the same message and you are married, then you probably aren't reading this book. If you did hear from God and the other person didn't, then it wasn't God. It might be time to reevaluate your view of who your Heavenly Father is and realize that perhaps you are wanting something so bad, you have put it in your head that God wants it too.

See Appendix: Voice of God Dater for a real life illustration

The Serial Dater

She is in back to back to back relationships. Keeping up with who she is dating is like always trying to have the latest smartphone.

The Gopher

Similar to the serial dater, this person pops up for community with other believers between dating relationships. You won't see them unless they are single and their dating lives are a mess.

The Ticking Clock
It's the woman who feels she is getting up there and won't have a chance to have a baby unless she gets married yesterday.

The Gifter
He really thinks that his abundance of gifts will sustain his relationship over the long haul. He has no capacity for intimacy and replaces it with presents.

Ice-Queen
She has a hardened heart and everyone knows what is invisibly but boldly stamped on her forehead.

Juicy Couture
She has daddy's money and always will have daddy's money. She has an expectation of living the pomp lifestyle. Any man who can't provide a proper standard of living will be expected to play by daddy's rules so that Juicy can have her things.

Emoto-man
He relates far better with women than with men. He isn't gay, but always has a posse of women around. He doesn't date any of them, because he always finds something wrong with them, and lives in fear of commitment.

I initially wrote most of these dating types to avoid to be funny. And then it hit me. I think at one time or another I was those dating types you would avoid. My ex-girlfriends would attest to it. They knew me well. Very well. Embarrasingly well. The reality is that if everything came out at once of how I ruined relationships with my conceit, pride, and lust you would scoff at picking up this book.

However, if I knew the stuff you had done in action or in thought, I would judge you just the same. I think the reality has got to come to this place that without dependence on Christ you are one of those messed up dating types. You are, because I am. We need Jesus.

Matt Chandler, a pastor here in the Dallas area, spoke at a Desiring God conference April 9, 2009 that spoke to my heart on why most dating books fail. They don't take into account that we are all jacked up beyond recognition—even if we think we're not.

He told a story of building a relationship with a 26 year old single mom who was dating a married man. He somehow got her to come to church by being a bit shady. He told her there was a concert that one of his friends was playing in. She agreed to go. It was true. His friend played, but then a pastor of some sort got up to speak. And this is where Chandler lost it.

"The minister got up and said we would talk about sex. I immediately go uh-oh..this could be a problem.

"He took a red rose, smelled it, and showed how pretty it was and threw it out in the crowd. 'Smell the rose, I want you to see the texture in it.' And then he began to teach.

"He then began one of the worst, most horrific handlings of what sex is and what it isn't that I ever sat through. It was fear mongering at its best. It was "You don't want syphilis do you? Everyone is smiling and having a good time until there is herpies on your lip!..."

Matt sat there in horror and kept thinking to himself, "What are you doing?" As he closed his message the minister asked that the rose be brought up to the stage. Some kid ran forward with a tattered, broken, petal less rose that had been clearly handled. He lifted up the rose, and asked the audience of about 1000, "Who would want this? Who would want this rose?"

Matt recounted his feelings.

"I remember feeling like real legitimate, "I want to hurt him, anger." And it was all I could do not to scream out, "Jesus wants the rose!" That's the point of the gospel: That Jesus wants the rose. That He made Him Who knew no sin to be sin on our behalf that we may become the righteousness of God that while we were yet sinners, Christ died for us. You are not even teaching the basics of our faith!"

See this sermon excerpt at
http://www.youtube.com/watch?v=o-zR3h2UsR4

So I want you to pause and reflect about the broken state of your existence. Not so you can rule yourself out of ever being datable, but so that you can look at the One who came for you and cry out, "Save me!"

It is from that perspective that I want you to read the rest of this book—Not as someone who just needs a tip or two to get the one. I want you to read the rest of this book as someone dependent on the mercy of God. Someone who fully knows the broken state in which Jesus found you, and is ready to go after a partner who is set on telling a broken world that Jesus came for them.

section four

DESCRIPTIVE, NOT PRESCRIPTIVE
BIBLICAL RELATIONSHIPS

Playing Call of Duty Modern Warfare doesn't make you a real warrior. Watching the Discovery Channel document Ranger School doesn't make you a Ranger. Watching G.I. Jane doesn't make you a Seal.

However, studying the great warriors can give you insight into what makes a great warrior, a great warrior. We can also learn from the mistakes that they made to get to the place where they were proficient in battling the enemy.

Watching *Dancing with the Stars* doesn't teach you how to dance. What I've learned from that show is that anyone can dance and depending how much practice and training one has, it makes a huge difference in their capacity to perform.

You have watched disaster after disaster in your own dating life and in the lives of others to know that it is not exactly child's play. I've also been to single's conference after single's conference watching people flounder around in their opinions. They had pretty decent principles. The problem was that the exegesis was flawed.

We take certain verses and give more emphasis to them, and we create a principle that fits with current culture and we are content to call that Biblical. In Seminary, we learned that was called eisegesis: Reading a meaning into a text that was never there or intended to be there.

I want to walk you through all the relationships where we see God giving us details of how a husband and wife came together. Some are great examples of how to pursue marriage, some are horrific, and some just happened. One that we won't go into is Mary and Joseph. Although they are a great couple to emulate, we meet them after they are engaged. Joseph's amazing strength and courage for not only marrying Mary after he found out she was pregnant, but his capacity for purity to ensure a virgin birth was believed by all are impressive. Unfortunately, we don't get much dating insight from them or even how they operated their marriage.

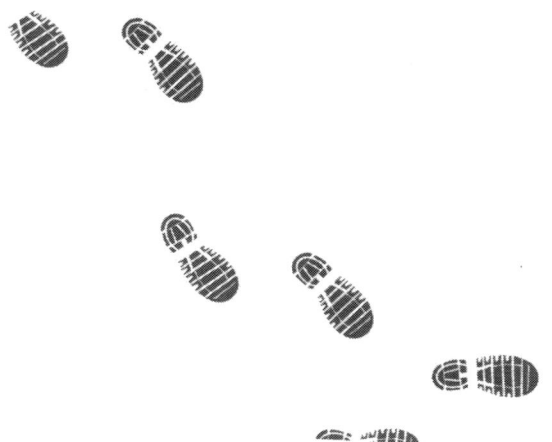

chapter nine:
ISAAC AND REBEKAH

Genesis 24 started with Abraham getting up there in years. He called in his chief of staff Eliezer and told them plainly, "Hey pal, get my boy a wife, but don't get him a Canaanite, but rather get him someone from our own family back in Aram Naharaim."

Eliezer headed off to the Old Country with a whole truck load of gifts and treasures, because the only way you are going to get a woman to leave her own family to go off with some foreigner guy was by having a lot of cash.

Eliezer loved Abraham and didn't want to screw this up. He prayed like crazy for God to help him find a wife who was willing to go back with him, because let's be honest here, I don't care how much money some weirdo has, a woman who doesn't know you from Adam isn't just going to hop on your camel and say, "Giddy up! To my husband!" unless she has some serious psychiatric issues or God told her to. So Eliezer went into town and started praying.

Genesis 24:12-14 (NIV)
Then he prayed, "O LORD, God of my master Abraham,
give me success today, and show kindness to my master
Abraham. See, I am standing beside this spring, and the
daughters of the townspeople are coming out to draw water.
May it be that when I say to a girl, 'Please let down your jar
that I may have a drink,' and she says, 'Drink, and I'll water
your camels too'—let her be the one you have chosen for your
servant Isaac. By this I will know that you have shown kindness to my master."

Observation/Interpretation:
This is a tough prayer to pray. This can be where some people try
to coerce God into getting something. I've prayed prayers like, "Dear
God, please make the next woman I see who wears blue and has
blue eyes be *the one.*"

God answered this prayer exactly as he prayed. Many have taken
this to mean that we need to pray for a specific spouse or for a
specific action to find *the one.* Maybe—but I think the point of that
was to see that Eliezer sought God and communicated with him
and walked by complete faith trusting that God would provide for
Abraham.

After this prayer, Rebekah showed up with a jar to fill up on
some water. The first thing that Eliezer noticed was her beauty. To
me, that's funny. The Bible is supposed to have men that look for
character qualities who ask things like, "Is this the kind of girl that
doesn't have a ton of issues and would get along with Isaac and has
a heart for God?" and all that, but no—she was hot.

He then found out that she was a virgin. I don't know how he
found this out. I always think of some guy with one of those wish-
bone water sticks walking around trying to find a virgin, and the
stick kept pointing at Rebekah. I'm sure I'm totally off, but that's in
my head.

Asking the other people at the well if she was a good girl may have
been the apt approach. Reputation always precedes a person in small
towns.

Apparently, it was true that she was a virgin, and it definitely took some sort of good family and good character traits to be a virgin. Eliezer felt she was qualified for him to inquire further.

Anyway, here's what happened,

Genesis 24:17 (NIV)

"The servant hurried to meet her and said, "Please give me a little water from your jar."

Observation/Interpretation

I wonder if Rebekah was freaked out by his approach. She went to the watering hole every day, and she pretty much knew everyone there. Men in this culture didn't talk to women because that was not culturally acceptable. So this random man ran to Rebekah and asked for water—like he couldn't just get his own—and here's Rebekah's response.

Genesis 24:18-21 (NIV)

"Drink, my lord," she said, and quickly lowered the jar to her hands and gave him a drink. After she had given him a drink, she said, "I'll draw water for your camels too, until they have finished drinking." So she quickly emptied her jar into the trough, ran back to the well to draw more water, and drew enough for all his camels. Without saying a word, the man watched her closely to learn whether or not the LORD had made his journey successful.

Observation/Interpretation

Eliezer turned "stalker" on Rebekah. After asking her to get him some water, he just stared and watched her. Eerie, I know, and maybe that was why she got some water for his camels as well. Who knows why, but God answered Eliezer's prayer exactly as he prayed. Eliezer made the next move.

Genesis 24:22 (NIV)

When the camels had finished drinking, the man took out a gold nose ring weighing a beka and two gold bracelets weighing ten shekels.

Genesis 24:25
> And she added, "We have plenty of straw and fodder, as well as room for you to spend the night. Then the man bowed down and worshiped the LORD.

Observation/Interpretation

Either Rebekah was a gold digger or she really had a servant's heart. I am going to lean toward the servant heart aspect here. Her family upbringing paid off, and she was overly kind to strangers. But it definitely didn't hurt Isaac's cause that this man came with a lot of cash.

The servant then asked about her family and if he could stay with them. It turned out she was a relative, and she knew how to take care of a man. Pretty good deal. So in less than an hour into the land of Abraham's relatives, Eliezer had a prospect and moved in to ink the deal.

Rebekah ran back to her brother Laban and told him what happened. Evidently, the father was not around anymore and Laban was the man of the house. Laban greeted him and asked Eliezer to come in and eat, and he went. Before he touched his food, he made his intentions clear. "I want to take your sister to my master's son for a wife."

Laban realized this was from the Lord and said, "Of course," to which Eliezer responded in worship to God.

Genesis 24:52-53 (NIV)
> When Abraham's servant heard what they said, he bowed down to the ground before the LORD.

Observation/Interpretation

Abraham's servant then convinced the family that Rebekah needed to leave right then and there, and the two of them headed back to the land of Canaan.

Meanwhile, back at the ranch, Isaac was doing his normal thing of drawing close to God daily. He probably knew that his father's servant would be out looking for his wife, but he didn't seem to worry about the time. He went about his day meditating on how great God was, since no Bibles existed yet for him to read.

Genesis 24:63 (NIV)

He went out to the field one evening to meditate, and as he looked up, he saw camels approaching.

Observation/Interpretation

And that was when it happened. The whole finding Rebekah issue was transparent to him. He knew that his father Abraham had the search committee out looking for his wife, and so he could rest in that. His dad had never let him down before. Sure his dad had strapped him up to some wood one day to kill him, but angels did stop him, so he knew that his dad had a direct line to God for things concerning him. If God wanted to build a line through him, he could take care of it through the intervention of angels if need be. He knew that he was loved and chosen.

Observation/Interpretation:

Having people praying like their life depends on it to find a wife for you is very helpful. How many of our friends are diligently searching for our husband or wife? Of course this was the servant's job. So perhaps those dating agencies are biblical after all. If there is a Christian matchmaker who really gets to know you and then prays like their life depends on it to find a spouse for you—that is biblical as well. Eliezer would thank God right on the spot anytime a prayer was answered. I mean that is a dedicated guy, a little weird with public prostration, but dedicated nevertheless. His heart was right.

Finally, notice how Isaac truly trusted his father Abraham and his Heavenly Father for a wife. This constant and regular communion with God was powerful in his finding a wife, which is why Moses mentioned he is out praying just before Eliezer brought Rebekah.

APPLICATION

- Find a trusted Christian friend who will diligently pray for your spouse and perhaps even search for your spouse.

- Pray in preparation for a spouse. God wants you to focus on Him in the midst of waiting for your spouse.

- Find a spouse in community. In other words don't date anyone that isn't known by your circle of friends, family, or mentors—if you don't have that, get it.

Praying For Your Future Husband

A friend of mine blogged this recently.

I've begun questioning whether we should encourage youth or single adults to pray for their future husband. After all, how do you pray for someone when you don't know their prayer requests or if they even exist? They might not. Since when is marriage the "be all, end all" of life? I've definitely fallen into the thinking pattern that it is. True love is the point of it all, right? Maybe wrong. That is a very worldly concept when you look at Jesus' life. And especially when you read Paul's letter to the Corinthians. Marriage is more of a bonus than a goal. So praying about it before there's a possibility it would happen is sort of like praying for a BMW.

I used to think Paul was crazy for suggesting we don't marry. I assumed a girl had broken his heart, and he was bitter. Now his suggestion is coming into focus. I'm starting to believe that loving someone on this earth with that eros kind of love is our way of crying out to God, longing to love Him in this way but feeling we can't because he is not physically in our midst. In this sense, marriage is a symbolic and desperate thing we do.

I'm not Paul. I'm not saying we should all stop getting married and start evangelizing. You can definitely do both. But I will say sorry to you, my future husband, for I am not praying for you daily, or really ever. It just weirds me out. I hope you understand.

I don't think praying about anything is ever wrong. I do agree with my friend's premise. My reasoning might be different. She looked at marriage like a BMW—an awesome bonus to an otherwise glorious life in Christ.

Here is where I differ. I wasn't made to be single. I can say that now that I am married. When I was single, I was on Facebook stalking every girl I was friends with trying to decipher if that person might be *the one*. Don't judge; you've done it too. You probably just paused stalking long enough to read this.

But here is the deal, and my wife will attest to this. I wasn't ready to be married until I prayed for my wife. I put ridiculous standards up for women to meet. The way they looked had to be a certain way. I conformed to the culture on that. The way they treated me had to be a certain way...kind of along the lines of June Cleaver.

They had to have a certain level of style, they had to have a certain ability to converse about politics or know who Michael Medved is. They had to have a love for Chicago Sports Teams and join me screaming "Da Bears! Da Bears! DA BEARS!" when they are on and not think that's weird. Their hair had to have a certain look. Look I'm not kidding...and for some of you, you can pick up your jaw at my shallowness or the fact that I just read your mail.

So here is what happened to me. I started really praying that God would bring me a wife. I realized that it wasn't good for me to be alone. I needed a partner. I needed a companion. I needed to have sex. I needed a completion to what God had said in the garden wasn't perfect in a perfect world. I needed a wife. So I asked him.

I really asked him. I used to pray for God to bring me a wife like most guys dream up their favorite sports cars on the corvette website. I wanted this much horsepower, these kinds of curves, this kind of gas mileage and so on. But this time, I prayed that God would bring me a wife.

One for me.

Not one that I would order out of a magazine, but a life partner that only God as my perfect Father would know.

Here is what happened. I toned down my view of women. It went from a runway model meets Mother Theresa to a woman filled with the Spirit ready to do ministry. God changed my heart.

So I prayed specifically that God would bring me the right *one*. It turned out I already knew her. Weird right?

APPLICATION

- Pray for your spouse. Pray for God to bring you not what you want, but who would be His best fit.

chapter ten:
JACOB & RACHEL
(AND LEAH)

Most view Jacob's relationship with Rachel as something that could have been set up in Hollywood. And therein lies the problem. In fact, many get caught up in Jacob's ability to wait for Rachel as opposed to the fact that he didn't seek God what-so-ever on this matter. In contrast to his father Isaac who meditated and prayed while his wife was being sought, Jacob hooked up with the first woman he saw. Let's get into the story.

Genesis 29 opened with Jacob heading off to the East. He was about 450 miles from home, safe from his brother's murderous threats but far from his mother's coddling. He rolled up to Haran and ran into folks from the area. He asked them if they knew Laban, Rebekah's brother. The men responded that Laban lived near and was doing well. His daughter Rachel was on her way with some sheep. Jacob then asked the men why they didn't lift the big rock off the well so that Rachel can water her sheep. The men answered that they wanted their sheep to get some water, and their sheep weren't there yet. So Jacob ignored the town tradition, rolled away the rock, watered Rachel's sheep, and then moved in for a kiss.

No other place in the Bible, save Song of Solomon, is there any talk of kissing. But here, Jacob moved by Rachel's beauty and the fact that she was someone he could marry. He went in for a kiss. Now culturally this had to cause a stir. Even today, you don't hear many men walking up to a girl at a gas station, paying for her gas and then playing tonsil hockey. So think back almost 4000 years and you can guess how well that went over with the locals as they watched this thing unfold.

So let's recap Jacob for a moment. He deceived his father, Isaac, for Esau's blessing. Esau swore to kill Jacob, and Jacob ran away to Haran on the advice of his mother. No prayer involved. God gave him a little revelation on his way out that He was with him with the whole dream of angels ascending and descending, but we have no interpretation of what that meant or what Jacob thought it meant. He traveled 450 miles and we have no record of him praying. He got to Haran and met Rachel, saw her beauty, broke tradition of uncovering the water well, gave a drink to Rachel's sheep, made out with her, and then cried. This is like uncovering the original chic flick.

The weird thing was that he told Rachel he was related to her after they made out. Jacob and Rachel immediately headed home; Laban got excited that his nephew showed up. They all have a month long party, and Jacob was treated like a guest. Eventually, there came a time where Laban, a shrewd businessman who knew nobody works for free, asked Jacob to name his price.

Jacob's price was Laban's daughter. Laban was no idiot and milked the deal for all it was worth. He demanded 7 years for Jacob to marry Rachel. Jacob was all about it. Now the thing that Jacob didn't realize was that he met his match as a trickster. There was no way Laban would marry off the second daughter without marrying off the first. And so he conspired with Leah for the switcheroo. This of course was reminiscent of the trick that Rebekah, Laban's sister, worked out with Jacob for him to get Esau's blessing. What goes around comes around, friends.

Again, there was a contrast between Isaac as a young man of prayer and Jacob as a young man who depended on his own intellect and cunning to get what he desired. This time he paid for it. The morning after the wedding, Jacob realized he had been had, and he actually married Leah.

Jacob did not divorce Leah, but rather made a deal for Rachel. He must work another 7 years for her.

It wasn't until Genesis 31 that Jacob communicated with God at all. In fact, God came to him. In this family, only Rachel and Leah prayed at all. They aren't praying for God's will, or to draw closer to him or to lead their lives, but rather they prayed for children.

Jacob could not have been a cruddier husband and leader of his family. He played favorites with his children and didn't love his family well. Although, when God told him to head back to Canaan, he obeyed. But what else would you do if God talked to you?

Jacob eventually reconciled with his brother, but the pattern of discord in his family would not end with him. His sons turned on Jacob's favorite son and sold him as a slave in Egypt. Through God-ordained circumstances, Jacob met up with his son who had risen from slave to prime minister. His son introduced him to Pharoah, and Pharoah asked him his age. Here was Jacob's response.

Genesis 47:9 ESV

"The days of the years of my sojourning are 130 years. Few and evil have been the days of the years of my life, and they have not attained to the days of the years of the life of my fathers in the days of their sojourning."

Not exactly the way I want to go out. God used his life. Through his family tree he brought about the redemption of the world. But he didn't spend his life seeking God. How did he go from weeping over finding Rachel to lamenting over his whole life? God used him for his purposes, but since he rarely sought God, he never found joy in the journey.

Observations of Jacob:

> He was hopeless romantic looking out only for himself and the desires of his eyes.

> He did not pray for where to go when he left Canaan.

> He did not pray for whom he should marry.

> He wanted to marry Rachel based solely on her beauty.

> Jacob never prayed and got a houseful of infighting that would later make him say to pharaoh in Genesis 47:9, "few and evil have been the years of my life..."

Interpretations:

> Jacob walked into the trap of having two wives because he never consulted God.

> God worked providentially through Jacob's prayerlessness.

Jacob, in spite of being fooled, did not divorce Leah. This was proper. Now of course, he ended up with essentially four wives and that does not translate to our contemporary world. What does translate is that although Jacob was deceived, he did not try to get out of that marriage.

Too many married people feel they were deceived. Not by their spouse's father, but by their spouse in presenting them to be something they never were. Divorce occurs. However, once you are married in the sight of God, it's a done deal.

> God uses sinful messed up people to fulfill his purposes.

No matter what mistakes a person makes, they can always be used by God. Jacob fulfilled the purpose of his life. In the end, his life didn't fulfill him. God did use him to start the nation of Israel and made them strong for 400 years in slavery in Egypt.

In an effort to control his circumstances, he made things

more difficult for himself. But God used a dysfunctional family with men and women whose faith did not necessarily reflect anything that we would want to imitate.

That gives me hope, because I can be pretty dysfunctional too.

APPLICATION

- You must diligently seek God to find a spouse.

- Once the "I do's" are exchanged, it's done.

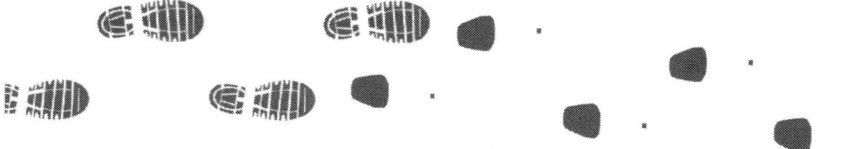

chapter eleven:
BOAZ & RUTH

Ruth proposed to Boaz in Ruth 3:9. Most argue that women must be passive in their role as a woman in their dating role. The Bible begs to differ.

Ruth was a Moabitess who had married Mahlon, the son of Elimelech and Naomi. Elimelech and his sons, Mahlon and Kilion, died leaving Naomi, Ruth, and her sister-in-law in Moab without a man to provide for them. Naomi told her daughters-in-law that she can't have any more sons for them to marry, so they should go back to their own houses and find new husbands. The sister-in-law agreed, but Ruth made a vow before God that she would never leave Naomi and swore her life to her. In that moment, Ruth made Naomi's God, Yahweh, her God. The Israelites would become her people forever, and she and Naomi returned to Bethlehem.

Naomi bewailed her situation. She moaned that God had forsaken her by taking all the men she loved out of her life. She looked at what was left and decided she was cursed.

Ruth, on the other hand, never bemoaned her situation, but was ready to work to provide for her mother-in-law and headed right to a field to pick up grain for Naomi when she entered Bethlehem. She went out to the field to glean wheat, essentially the process of gathering the excess crops left over by the landowner, which was actually a way of helping out the poor by giving them a chance to gather their own food.

It just so happened that Ruth worked Boaz's field. Boaz took notice of her and made sure his men treated her well. Ruth reported to Naomi how she received special treatment from Boaz, and Naomi knew that he was interested. Better than his interest, Boaz was a relative.

There was no Levitical law that stated that a near relative had the duty to marry another dead relative's widow. However, property rights were an issue. Naomi, as a woman, could not own property, but a man could own the property for her and make sure she was provided for. This was common knowledge, but who would do it wasn't.

My wife is always quick to point out that Boaz actually made the first move here. He was the one who showed interest. He was the one that makes it clear he was interested in her by being overly kind. She wasn't the only servant girl in the gang, but she was always favored.

Naomi then schemed with Ruth when she found out about Boaz's interest. She told Ruth to put on her best clothes, perfume, and make-up and then go down to the threshing floor (the place where the wheat was separated from the chaff). Then she told Ruth to do something very strange. After Boaz had his fill of wine, she told Ruth to "uncover his feet" and lie down and wait for Boaz to tell her what to do. Now, this is where the Bible goes euphemistic—you know, using an inoffensive word to describe something, how shall we say?—private.

We know when Saul went into the cave to relieve himself in 1 Samuel 24:3 the verse literally reads "cover his feet." We know this because Saul goes into a cave and goes "number one," as it's clearly stated in the following verses of 1 Samuel 24.

When Naomi told Ruth to get all dressed up, wait for Boaz to get fat and happy on food and wine, and then uncover his feet, what could she possibly have meant? Ruth 3:4 is translated several ways. Only the New English Translation and the Message are bold enough to make a stab at explaining the meaning of "uncover his feet." The NET used his legs which would get kind of risqué, and the Message is flat out saying that "uncovering his feet" means, "I want to get married."

Ruth 3:4			
NASV	NET	ESV	Message
"It shall be when he lies down, that you shall notice the place where he lies, and you shall go and **uncover his feet** and lie down; then he will tell you what you shall do."	When he gets ready to go to sleep, take careful notice of the place where he lies down. Then go, **uncover his legs,** and lie down beside him. He will tell you what you should do."	When he lies down, note the place where he is lying. Then go and **uncover his feet** and lie down. He will tell you what to do."	Lie at his feet **to let him know that you are available to him for marriage.** Then wait and see what he says. He'll tell you what to do.

Ruth's actions reveal Naomi's intentions. In Ruth 3:8 Boaz had a good time, got a lil tipsy, and fell asleep. On cue, Ruth quietly followed.

Ruth 3:8		
NASV	NET	Message
and [Ruth] **uncovered his feet and lay down.** It happened in the middle of the night that the man was startled and bent forward; and behold, a woman was **lying at his feet.** He said, "Who are you?" And she answered, "I am Ruth your maid. So **spread your covering over your maid, for you are a close relative."**	[She] **uncovered his legs, and lay down beside him.** In the middle of the night he was startled and turned over. **Now he saw a woman lying beside him!** He said, "Who are you?" She replied, "I am Ruth, your servant. **Marry your servant, for you are a guardian of the family interests."**	She **lay down to signal her availability for marriage.** In the middle of the night the man was suddenly startled and sat up. Surprise! **This woman asleep at his feet!** He said, "And who are you?" She said, "I am Ruth, your maiden; **take me under your protecting wing. You're my close relative, you know, in the circle of covenant redeemers—you do have the right to marry me."**

Observation/Interpretation:

There were several things that Ruth did here when she made this request. She laid down by his side and when Boaz woke up she asked him a question. The direct translation of the Hebrew is "spread your wing over your servant."

In Ezekiel 16:8, the Lord metaphorically spread his "kanaf" over a naked woman representing Israel as an act of protection and marriage. Depending on what version of the Bible you have, it is translated as "corner of the garment" or "skirt." The actual word "kanaf" means "wing" or "extremity." So in Ezekiel, the Lord put Israel under his protective wing. Here Ruth asked Boaz to do the same thing for her.

Ruth, for the most part, would have been looked down upon for this, right? I mean this was scandalous. She approached a very respected God-fearing man in the middle of the night and made an advance to marry him. So what did Boaz think of her move?

Ruth 3:10-14 (NET)

> He said, "May you be rewarded by the LORD, my dear! This act of devotion is greater than what you did before. For you have not sought to marry one of the young men, whether rich or poor. Now, my dear, don't worry! I intend to do for you everything you propose, for everyone in the village knows that you are a worthy woman.
>
> Now yes, it is true that I am a guardian, but there is another guardian who is a closer relative than I am. Remain here tonight. Then in the morning, if he agrees to marry you, fine, let him do so. But if he does not want to do so, I promise, as surely as the LORD lives, to marry you. Sleep here until morning." So she slept beside him until morning. She woke up while it was still dark.
>
> Boaz thought, "No one must know that a woman visited the threshing floor."

Observation/Interpretation:

Boaz viewed Ruth's move as an action of grace upon her mother-in-law, Naomi. He saw her seeking him as a provider for her and Naomi as something very noble. Boaz used the Hebrew word "Ha-eel." He described her with the same words written in Proverbs 31:10 to describe the woman of noble character.

She was called that for going after Boaz when she could have gone after one of the younger men implying that she could have chosen to ask one of the younger men to marry her.

This brings us to an interesting place. In a culture that didn't allow women to even be in a men's public place like the threshing floor, Ruth was considered an incredibly good woman.

Why?

Her heart was to provide for her mother in law by choosing a respectable established man like Boaz for her husband.

Clearly Boaz was righteous because it doesn't appear that he took advantage of Ruth and "married her" on the spot. He submitted to the cultural norm of giving the man who had the closest relationship to Ruth the opportunity to marry her. Remember what was at stake here was Naomi's property which whoever marries Ruth inherits. There was no Biblical precedence for this practice, for nowhere in the Torah did it say anything about anyone other than brothers marrying a dead brother's widow to carry on the name of the deceased brother although this is exactly what Boaz does. In fact, Matthew and Luke include Boaz in the lineage of Jesus in their gospels.

I am not saying that men should go to bed every night expecting to wake up to the woman God has for him. But what I am saying is that we may have boxed ourselves in too tightly with this Medieval knight concept that the men are supposed to pursue their princess. They are to win the princess and take her on his great adventure.

In this model, the woman went after a husband. She asked that man to be her covering and to be responsible for her. She also made it clear that she was willing to be obedient to his leadership and there are no misconceptions of expectations. The woman was clearly joining that man's world to be his helpmate and was not being swept off her feet to have all her romantic dreams come true.

This kind of reminds me of the way Adrienne and I started dating. She didn't come to me in the middle of the night, uncover my legs, and lay down, but she had started to feel that I was interested. We lived in adjacent apartment complexes and I loved spending time with her. I texted. I called. I went running with her. I sought out every opportunity to be with her.

Adrienne, feeling the sense that she was falling for me, but being raised properly that a woman didn't pursue a man made me an offer that forced me to make a decision. We had just gone running and we went to get something to eat. At Jason's Deli she said she had to say something to me.

She stuck a fork in her salad and said, "Chris, I am really enjoying my time with you. However, I can't hang out with you any longer if we aren't dating. I can't guard my heart."

The DTR. Adrienne wanted to define the relationship. Not quite as bold as Ruth, but I felt it was right up there.

My response to that was a kind of shock that a woman would be that bold. But it made me think. All of a sudden, I realized that I loved being with her. I loved the way she worked. I loved the way we talked. I was definitely attracted to her.

I took time to think about it. We had both planned to be on an I am Second mission trip to Bolivia. We were partnered together planting churches. After seeing her work among the locals in Bolivia, I was hooked. When we got back, we started officially dating.

APPLICATION

- Men, initiate with women by showing interest.

- Women, respond to initiation with clarification of that interest.

- Define the relationship so that both the man and the woman know exactly where each stands.

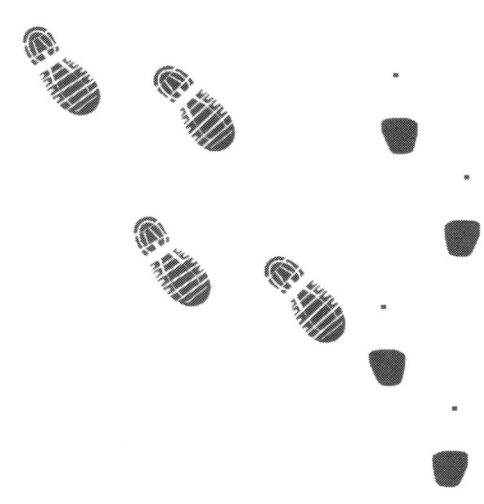

chapter twelve:
DAVID & ABIGAIL

In 1 Samuel 25, David and his men are on the run from Saul. They depended on the good-natured Israelites to support them. In return, David provided security to sheep herders. In this chapter, we find David watching over the sheep of Nabal, a crotchety old man. David asked if he could have some bread for his men, and Nabal gave him the finger. That made David angry enough to kill him.

On the way to take Nabal's life, David ran into Abigail. She knew of her husband's hot temper and looked to mediate on his behalf. Abigail heard how good David had been to Nabal, and how her husband had insulted David. She knew she had to act fast because impending doom for Nabal and his whole family would soon come if she didn't quell David's anger.

Abigail grabbed two hundred loaves of bread, a couple bottles of wine, five racks of lamb, grain, and dessert enough to feed all of David's men. She loaded up the buffet on donkeys and headed to meet David.

Upon finding him, she dismounted her donkey and bowed before him. She said,

1 Samuel 25:24 (NIV)
"My lord, let the blame be on me alone. Please let your servant to speak to you; hear what your servant has to say. May my lord pay no attention to that wicked man Nabal. He is just like his name—his name is Fool, and folly goes with him. But as for me, your servant, I did not see the men my master sent.

"Now since the LORD has kept you, my master, from bloodshed and from avenging yourself with your own hands, as surely as the LORD lives and as you live, may your enemies and all who intend to harm my master be like Nabal. And let this gift, which your servant has brought to my master, be given to the men who follow you.

"Please forgive your servant's offense, for the LORD will certainly make a lasting dynasty for my master, because he fights the LORD's battles. Let no wrongdoing be found in you as long as you live.

Even though someone is pursuing you to take your life, the life of my master will be bound securely in the bundle of the living by the LORD your God. But the lives of your enemies he will hurl away as from the pocket of a sling.

When the LORD has done for my master every good thing he promised concerning him and has appointed him leader over Israel, my master will not have on his conscience the staggering burden of needless bloodshed or of having avenged himself. And when the LORD has brought my master success, remember your servant."

Observation/Interpretation:
Wow. Abigail used her knowledge of David and the fact that he was to be king, along with knowing that he served the Lord to assuage David's anger. She tempered his anger and saved her family. Here Abigail did several things to impress David.
  ➤ She took responsibility for the folly of her family

➢ She provided the gifts that her husband should have provided

➢ She acknowledged David's right to reign

➢ She acknowledged all that David had done in fighting the Lord's enemies.

➢ Abigail saved her family with this speech.

Back to the story. David's response showed how well she spoke and the effect that she had on David.

1 Samuel 25:32-36 (NIV)
David said to Abigail, "Praise be to the LORD, the God of Israel, who has sent you today to meet me. May you be blessed for your good judgment and for keeping me from bloodshed this day and from avenging myself with my own hands.

Otherwise, as surely as the LORD, the God of Israel, lives, who has kept me from harming you, if you had not come quickly to meet me, not one male belonging to Nabal would have been left alive by daybreak."

Then David accepted from her hand what she had brought him and said, "Go home in peace. I have heard your words and granted your request."

Observation/Interpretation:
David saw in this woman incredible character and courage. She could have easily been afraid and hidden, but she took responsibility for her family. She protected her husband who would have died and was loyal to him, even though he was fool. That was huge. A man needs a woman who will follow him even though he is an idiot. He may not even know he needs that, but here David witnessed a woman saving her family.

Ten days after this incident, the Lord struck Nabal and killed him. Upon hearing the news, David sent word for her to become his bride. Not exactly the most romantic proposal—but a proposal nevertheless. We have to remember the times, chivalry hadn't hit yet, so the fact that David even sent a proposal is something to admire. Not only that, but David sent the limo with his security detachment to pick her up to become his bride.

Her response further revealed her character.

1 Samuel 25:40-42 (NIV)

> She bowed down with her face to the ground and said, "Here is your maidservant, ready to serve you and wash the feet of my master's servants."
>
> Abigail quickly got on a donkey and, attended by her five maids, went with David's messengers and became his wife.

Observation/Interpretation:

From Abigail's first encounter with David, she showed him nothing but respect. He saw an intelligent, graceful, responsible woman. Any king that sees a woman with that much going for her is going to throw down a marriage proposal as soon as she is available.

Abigail came to David ready to serve him and his mission. She was willing to do the most debasing things to serve her husband.

This may not seem like the best description of a marriage (that whole polygamy thing gets awkward to talk about). David saw her character when married to another man. He knew what she was about and how she would handle pressure. He saw a strength that few women possessed.

APPLICATION

- Verify your potential mate's response to pressure.

Do ministry alongside your potential mate and watch how she handles pressure.

Watch to see if your potential mate averts blame or takes responsibility. Is she willing to take responsibility for others? That is a powerful testimony for what kind of woman she is.

chapter thirteen:
SOLOMON & THE SHULAMITE

The Song of Solomon has always amazed me with the way that this book celebrated sex. There is no talk of having babies and keeping things PG. Sex and romantic love are celebrated as gifts from God.

Some have come from Christian homes where they depicted sex as something no one talked about. The church didn't talk about it, and anything sexual was super taboo.

Most evangelicals have come to the conclusion that sex is not only a part of pro-creation, it is something that should be celebrated. I think that is a welcomed change.

For the single person reading this book of the Bible, beware. It definitely wouldn't fit on any contemporary conservative Christian dating bookshelf. I mean, it started off with the woman wanting to suck face with her man. She wasn't trying to fain or hide her interest. She was making no attempts at being quiet and waiting for the man to pursue her. She made her wants and desires known. She was ready to go.

Chapter 1

Verse one starts off by titling the book. Essentially it could be retitled "King Solomon's Greatest Hit." 1 Kings 4:32 told us that Solomon wrote 1005 songs. He was a lyrical master and this was one of his most prolific.

A woman broke on the scene in verse two and started by sharing her very deep affection for her non-husband. In most Bibles the speaker is denoted in the margin or super-scripted. That wasn't in the original text; however, it does help in better understanding the song.

Song of Solomon 1:2-4a (ESV)
> Let him kiss me with the kisses of his mouth! For your love is better than wine; your anointing oils are fragrant; your name is oil poured out; therefore virgins love you. Draw me after you; let us run. The king has brought me into his chambers.

Observation/Interpretation:
So I feel like I just walked in on an awkward conversation of a woman whispering sweet nothings in her man's ear. She wanted to play tonsil hockey. She noticed he smelled great, and his name (or a better word might be reputation) preceded him. He was the complete package of attractive and well-thought-of by everyone. The NET Bible translates that last line as, "May the king draw me to his chambers," expressing the woman's desire to be his.

Song of Solomon 1:4b (ESV)
> We will exult and rejoice in you; we will extol your love more than wine; rightly do they love you.

Observation/Interpretation:
Here is a change in the character. The daughters of Jerusalem whom we will meet in the following verses are giving approval to the

romance. They are excited for her.

Song of Solomon 1:5-7 (ESV)
> I am very dark, but lovely, O daughters of Jerusalem,
> like the tents of Kedar, like the curtains of Solomon.
> Do not gaze at me because I am dark, because the sun
> has looked upon me. My mother's sons were angry with me;
> they made me keeper of the vineyards, but my own vineyard
> I have not kept!

Observation/Interpretation:
This woman responded to the daughters of Jerusalem with her insecurity. Her brothers gave her no special treatment and put her to work. We don't know why they had anger towards this woman, but they did. Her working on their vineyards didn't allow her to apply beauty treatments.

Her darkness would have made her feel insecure because she wasn't a typical woman of Solomon's court. Women in the Middle East wanted fair skin because that meant the woman was an indoor girl—a status symbol for the affluent.

Some take her brothers being angry with her as her being good with authority. She may have been great with authority. I can't imagine a woman in that day and age being courted by a king who didn't do well with authority, but this verse doesn't make that case.

It could in fact mean that she was rebellious and was punished often for her inability to respect authority. We don't have enough information here to draw any concrete conclusion.

Song of Solomon 1:7 (ESV)
> Tell me, you whom my soul loves, where you pasture
> your flock, where you make it lie down at noon; for why
> should I be like one who veils herself beside the flocks of
> your companions?

Observation/Interpretation:
The woman addressed her lover. Solomon was not a shepherd.

Kings in general don't hang out with sheep. In ancient Near Eastern love poems, a shepherd was common terminology for a man. She wanted to spend some quality time with Solomon, but she had standards. She would not be confused with a prostitute who just played the part of his fan club.

APPLICATION

- Men, you don't need a posse of women. It shows your lack of relationship with your dad and the fact that you find your security from women.

- Women, don't play the prostitute. I'm not just talking sex here. If you get the same emotional satisfaction from a guy that you would get from a boyfriend or spouse, you are setting yourself up to be either hurt or not pursued by another guy who would be interested.

Song of Solomon 1:8 (ESV)

If you do not know, O most beautiful among women, follow in the tracks of the flock, and pasture your young goats beside the shepherds' tents.

Observation/Interpretation:

Scholars debate who is speaking in this verse, but it seems that Solomon wouldn't chide her and tell her to do the very thing that would cause her to look like a prostitute. More likely it was the daughters of Jerusalem saying that if you don't believe you're gorgeous, you're crazy, and you might as well go back to the losers back home and miss out on the king.

Song of Solomon 1:9-10 (ESV)

I compare you, my love, to a mare among Pharaoh's chariots. Your cheeks are lovely with ornaments, your neck with strings of jewels.

Solomon affirmed her beauty by comparing her to a horse. Before you go feminist on Solomon here, just realize that there were only stallions (male horses) in Pharoah's army. Mares (female horses) were sent into the ranks to distract the stallions so that the other army might have an advantage in battle. So in other words, she is so fine, every man is staring, distracted by her beauty. He also admired her choice of jewelry. Apparently this woman shopped at Tiffany's.

Song of Solomon 1:11 (ESV)
    We will make for you ornaments of gold, studded with silver.

Observation/Interpretation:
    The daughters of Jerusalem come through for their friend and are going to hook her up with some bling to please the king.

Song of Solomon 1:12-14 (ESV)
    While the king was on his couch, my nard gave forth its fragrance. My beloved is to me a sachet of myrrh that lies between my breasts. My beloved is to me a cluster of henna blossoms in the vineyards of Engedi.

Observation/Interpretation:
    The couch that the king was on would be his banqueting table. It was common to have a couch like bench with pillows that allowed the king to sit up properly and eat. The word nard always made me think of something less than holy. But it turns out that it is a perfumed ointment that was common for women to wear in sachets around their necks. The sachet of myrrh was kinda like one of those smell-good things that people have hanging from their rear view mirror. Same concept—only on a person. She wore oils and impressed him with her smell. Remember, bathing wasn't exactly an everyday thing, so perfumes and oils covered up the nasty B.O.
    Her sachet of myrrh reminded her of him every time she breathed in the wonderful aroma. Then she commented that Solomon was like a cluster of henna blossoms that smelled like roses but also made a reddish-orange dye.

Song of Solomon 1:15 (ESV)
    Behold, you are beautiful, my love; behold, you are beauti-

ful; your eyes are doves.

Observation/Interpretation:

This is where I think Solomon was stalling as he was searching for adjectives, because instead of going on and on like the woman, he resorts to repeating himself. Quite possibly he is just lost in her eyes. Some want to make a big deal about how commenting on eyes meant that Solomon was really commenting on how wonderful her character was, but when was the last time you stared into a woman's eyes, complimented her on her physical beauty, and then thought about her character?

Song of Solomon 1:16 (ESV)

Behold, you are beautiful, my beloved, truly delightful.
Our couch is green; the beams of our house are cedar; our rafters are pine.

The woman recounted how wonderful it was to be with Solomon. She gave us details of the fact that they sat on a grassy field surrounded by trees—a gorgeous date for two. Now some commentators note that they are outside which proves they are in public. I somehow doubt that. Two lovers staring into each other's eyes are not going to want to be seen.

It's possible that they are being chaperoned. Perhaps the daughters of Jerusalem are watching nearby as Solomon and the Shulamite gawk at each other, but the scripture doesn't give us that information. Some assume that the king would never be alone and therefore was chaperoned. Again, tough to put into a 21st century context.

I'm not advocating here to take a girl to a secluded area on a first date and romance her and stare into her eyes and share every deep dark secret. However, I am going to argue that this scripture doesn't say anything about not going on a romantic date alone. I do think an argument can be made that the date wasn't secret.

APPLICATION

- Make sure your community knows you are going on a date.

Chapter 2

Song of Solomon 2:1-2 (ESV)

I am a rose of Sharon, a lily of the valleys.

As a lily among brambles, so is my love among the young women.

Observation/Interpretation:

The woman compares herself to a rose of Sharon which is like a Lily. Solomon responds back that the other women were like ugly brambles, compared to her beauty.

Song of Solomon 2:3-6 (ESV)

As an apple tree among the trees of the forest, so is my beloved among the young men. With great delight I sat in his shadow, and his fruit was sweet to my taste.

He brought me to the banqueting house, and his banner over me was love. Sustain me with raisins; refresh me with apples, for I am sick with love. His left hand is under my head, and his right hand embraces me!

Observation/Interpretation:

The Shulamite again got a mouthful of Solomon. Apples and raisins were often used as aphrodisiacs. With the way Solomon's hands are all over her body it is clear they are in full-fledged make out here.

The term "his banner over me was love" has been interpreted to mean that Solomon had marked his territory and was claiming her publicly—something like going F.B.O. However, other scholars argue that it is from an Akkadian word that meant desire or intent so the phrase would mean "his intent toward me is lovemaking."

It's tough to make a call either way on that one, but we can see three things pretty clearly. Sitting in the shadow of another denoted protection. The banner over her was a clear mark of public identification, and their closeness showed a deep intimacy.

Since no Israelite in their right mind would ever advocate sex before marriage, I can tell you that if the couple in this passage are having sex, then they are already married. If not, then they are deeply kissing one another with the man gripping her head and body passionately as they kiss.

Some have said that this is not her actually having sex or making out with her boyfriend, but rather her thinking about the wedding day.

If someone made this out to be a married couple, I wouldn't argue it. I'm not sure if I'm comfortable telling those that are dating, "Hey it's okay to fantasize about being married just don't do anything physically."

Remember the point of Song of Solomon was never to teach 21st century Christians how to date, but rather to celebrate sex and the romantic love that a man and a woman share.

Song of Solomon 2:7 (ESV)

> I adjure you, O daughters of Jerusalem, by the gazelles or the does of the field, that you not stir up or awaken love until it pleases.

Observation/Interpretation:

On the heels of a solid make out session, Solomon gave some advice here to all watching from the outside. He wanted them to be patient for love to come to them. Perhaps a better way to put this is he wanted them to be patient for sex. To get close to a skittish animal like an antelope or a deer one must be very patient. To get the real deal love, one must wait for it.

This verse is repeated in 3:5 and 8:4. It is the refrain of the song. It is a powerful verse that sums up how to get the kind of love that everyone wants. Be patient and wait.

Now it does seem odd that the woman who gave this advice is essentially drooling over Solomon and throwing herself at him. He wasn't exactly backing off. Patience seemed to be the last thing on the mind of this young woman.

Solomon realized the power of love and how intoxicating it will always be. Outside the confines and boundaries God prescribed, disaster will find you. He knew that once they gave in fully to it, it would be impossible to turn back.

We all have seen the carnage that becomes those who have tried to walk with the Lord and engage in sex outside God's gift of marriage. We have also seen celebrities making a mockery of marriage find themselves paying the price of hurt, heartbreak and broken families.

Purity matters. I know that some who read this grew up with an illicit sexual past. God knew that and saved you in spite of that. However, now is the time to learn a new step. You will have to think about it. You will have to be cautious and submit to some personal boundaries that may not make sense to others.

APPLICATION

- Make the relationship public. Facebook official (F.B.O.) is a great place to start.

- Check a man's reputation. Receive advice from friends and talk to them about how he treats you. Friends are a great sounding board to capture reality when in love.

- Wait until the proper time for sex, which is marriage.

Song of Solomon 2:8-13 (ESV)

The voice of my beloved! Behold, he comes, leaping over the mountains, bounding over the hills. My beloved is like a gazelle or a young stag. Behold, there he stands behind our wall, gazing through the windows, looking through the lattice.

My beloved speaks and says to me: "Arise, my love, my beautiful one, and come away, for behold, the winter is past; the rain is over and gone. The flowers appear on the earth, the time of singing has come, and the voice of the turtledove is heard in our land.

The fig tree ripens its figs, and the vines are in blossom; they give forth fragrance. Arise, my love, my beautiful one, and come away.

Observation/Interpretation:

The Shulamite heard her love coming to her. The scene has shifted to her home in Lebanon which we know from 4:8, 15. Her excitement is overwhelming as time has passed between the time she saw him last. Might have been a day, could have been a whole winter. But that is how love is. A day apart from the one you are in love with is an eternity.

The spring imagery that the Shulamite presented might be a look back at 2:7. Perhaps the time had come for their love to fully blossom. Solomon's request for her to come away is another chance for them to go on a walk or enjoy each other away from others.

Song of Solomon 2:14 (ESV)
> O my dove, in the clefts of the rock, in the crannies of the cliff, let me see your face, let me hear your voice, for your voice is sweet, and your face is lovely.

Observation/Interpretation:
Solomon sensed that the Shulamite, although excited to see him, might be tense with what is on her heart. He reminded her that he loved her, and that would never change. He encouraged her to come out and tell him what is on her heart. It was like coaxing a little dove out from the safety of the mountain cleft. There had to be a lot of trust for the bird to do that with a powerful man.

Solomon reminded her he wanted to hear her concerns and anything she said would be sweet as he sought to please her. Feeling secure, the Shulamite brought up some concerns.

Song of Solomon 2:15 (ESV)
> Catch the foxes for us, the little foxes that spoil the vineyards, for our vineyards are in blossom.

Observation/Interpretation:
The Shulamite gave it to him straight. She wanted him to take care of the issues that might be potential problems for their relationships. Foxes were seen in this time as the mischievous creature that would ruin vineyards or crops. The vineyards represented their ripening relationship. They were about to be fully bloomed in marriage and she wanted Solomon to take care of the issues so that they didn't spoil their marriage.

Some have thought that it was the other women in Solomon's court. Others have commented that it was arguments and things that they hadn't fully resolved yet. The audience wasn't let in on what the issues were, but the audience was informed upon whom the responsibility to catch the foxes fell—Solomon.

The man was responsible for getting to the heart of conflict and resolving any issues that might come between them

APPLICATION

- Men, initiate conflict resolution and prepare the way for deepening a ripening relationship for marriage.

- Women, vocalize concerns with a potential spouse. Let them resolve issues.

Song of Solomon 2:16-17 (ESV)
    My beloved is mine, and I am his; he grazes among the lilies.
    Until the day breathes and the shadows flee, turn, my beloved, be like a gazelle or a young stag on cleft mountains.

Observation/Interpretation
    The Shulamite remained convinced that he would take care of the problem and restated her security in his love. As a strong shepherd is with his flock among lilies, so will she be protected and cared for by this amazing man.

    She then shifted from expressing confidence in his character to expressing hope for their upcoming marriage. She expressed her desire for him to be like a gazelle or a young stag on cleft mountains—which is a rough translation from the mount of Bether. That literally means the space between the mountains which most scholars believe take that not as literal mountains, but, well, cleavage.

    She readied herself for the physical intimacy that followed a lifelong commitment. One can see a correlation between her confidence in Solomon's ability to lead her and her desire for physical intimacy.

Chapter 3

The first four verses of chapter three take us to the next scene. The Shulamite after expressing her confidence in Solomon, had a nightmare. Solomon couldn't be found. She ultimately found him. In the dream, she took Solomon back to her mother's bedroom, the safest place she could think of—to hold him until the wedding could be consummated.

Song of Solomon 3:5 (ESV)
   I adjure you, O daughters of Jerusalem, by the gazelles or the does of the field, that you not stir up or awaken love until it pleases.

This is the last phrase before the wedding processional. The end of their courtship had come. Their patience will finally pay off. This section ended with another clear warning from Solomon not to let love consume them until the proper time.

The wedding happened and life happened. They went through the excitement of exploring each others bodies. They went through the excitement of being newlyweds followed by the struggle of apathy. We find Solomon and the Shulamite struggling to love one another better. They long to bring back the desire they felt during their "dating."

Song of Solomon's overarching theme is that sex is something to be enjoyed and something that is to be enjoyed throughout the duration of a marriage. However, sex was never intended to be the ultimate thing, merely a good thing.

APPLICATION

- Sex is a good thing. Don't make it an ultimate thing.

chapter fourteen:
SAMSON & THE PHILISTINES

Samson was a great character in Israel's history because he was everything you wouldn't expect a super hero to be. He was great at doing one thing: destroying stuff. So one can imagine that when it came to relationships, he simply did what he always did: destroy them.

Samson is in Hebrews 11, the Hall of Faith, so there are definitely some things we should emulate about his relationship with the Lord, but when it comes to his relationship with people, you are pretty safe in doing the opposite of what Samson did.

Judges 14:1-3 (NASV)

> Then Samson went down to Timnah and saw a woman in Timnah, one of the daughters of the Philistines. So he came back and told his father and mother, "I saw a woman in Tim-

nah, one of the daughters of the Philistines; now therefore, get her for me as a wife."

Then his father and his mother said to him, "Is there no woman among the daughters of your relatives, or among all our people, that you go to take a wife from the uncircumcised Philistines?" But Samson said to his father, "Get her for me, for she looks good to me."

Samson was more than just a little direct with his parents. The part that makes me wince a little, beyond the way he talked to his parents, is that he wanted the one that looked good.

This relationship eventually ends in a divorce and the death of the woman and her father. But verse four gives us more insight into Samson's choice.

Judges 14:4 (NET)
    However his father and mother did not know it was of the Lord for He was seeking an opportunity to stir up trouble with the Philistines.

Observation/Interpretation
    In chapter thirteen we learn that the Israelites have done evil in the eyes of the Lord and the Philistines are sent to punish and rule over the Israelites. Finally, God sends the deliverer, Samson. He reminds me a bit of General Patton. He was a take-no-prisoners, break-glass-in-case-of-war kind of man. Everything he touched, he destroyed.

    And God wanted it like that. God was looking to exact his judgment through the vehicle of Samson. Here is where God actually ordained a relationship to fulfill his will to punish those who hurt Israel. Who says God can't use a bizarre relationship for His Glory?

Samson and Delilah

Eventually Samson married another Philistine hottie which would pave the way for more Philistines to die. She used her beauty and seduction to find out the secret to Samson's strength (his hair) and then she shaved his head and handed him over to the Philistine leaders. They gouged out his eyes and paraded him around the Philistine temple. Samson's hair grew again, and he killed 3,000 along with himself in one day by pushing down the temple pillars.

Again, I don't know if this teaches us anything other than if you marry a girl that is hot and wants nothing to do with your God, you will end up in trouble. It also teaches us that when a man is in love, it is almost impossible to stop him.

I can't imagine any of his friends (Did he have friends?) sitting him down and being like, "Samson, you really need to re-think this one."

No one would stop Samson from marrying the woman that would eventually destroy him. Here was a guy that God used completely to fulfill his will, but I wonder if God could have used him as a wise judge who fought Israel's enemies while having a stable family.

Samson was a man of great faith. He is in Hebrews 11 for a reason. It doesn't fully make sense to me, but God's ways are not my ways. I am just trying to glean as much as I can from the scripture about relationships, and I find that sometimes God has another agenda than the one we have mapped out for our lives.

We have to trust that God not only knows what He is doing, but He is going to get glory from our life and that ultimately it will be for our good.

Observations:

➢ God had an agenda for Samson's life.

➢ God empowered Samson with His Holy Spirit to go and fight Israel's enemies.

➢ Samson married Israel's enemy.

➢ Delilah led Samson to not only destroy Israel's enemy, but to destroy Samson.

➢ Samson didn't come close to following God's plan for marriage.

➢ Samson's faith was genuine, even though his execution may

have been flawed.

➤ Delilah enjoyed the power she had over Samson

➤ Delilah used the power she had over Samson for personal gain

Interpretations:

➤ Parents have a pretty good idea of who will be a good match for their children.

➤ Parents can't force you to marry or not to marry anyone.

➤ Some women love the power of making a strong man weak.

➤ Some women will seek to cause a godly man's downfall for the sake of personal gain.

➤ God gives us the power to fight our enemies.

➤ When we marry the enemy, we end up destroying ourselves.

➤ God is ultimately in control of our lives

➤ God will use our lives for His glory.

➤ The strongest warriors can be taken out by inward immorality.

APPLICATION

• Don't marry the enemy.

• Listen to your believing parents on whom to marry. Even if your parents aren't believers, they still have pretty good insight into your life.

Samson shows us one important lesson: God will get glory regardless of how you act.

You can be a wonderful bad example of what happens when godly men use their strength for their own lusts. God will use them, but it sure seems that they pay a huge price.

So here is the embarrassing part of my life coming out. When I was single, I was speaking at an 8,000 person church and I made eye contact with one of the pretty choir members. After I spoke, I signed books in the lobby, and she came by and thanked me for writing the book. At the time I couldn't grasp how she had already read my book, but I made a mental note of it and filed it away.

Later, I received an email from her, and we quickly started texting and Facebooking. Soon she was coming to visit. I picked her up from the airport, and she had her little dog that rode on the plane with her. Her matching pink luggage made me feel like she was a mini-Paris Hilton, but I overlooked it. She was super fun. In about an hour's time I was totally hooked on this woman. She was beautiful. If she had heard me speak, she knew how much I loved Jesus, and she wanted to come and sing for me at my events.

She then told me she had just received a $250,000 signing bonus from SONY records for her to be a pop star. So here I was with my jaw hanging staring at this woman. In my head, I went through a mental checklist. She was gorgeous. She loved what I did. She read my book and highlighted every part. She was loaded and wanted to support my ministry. What else was there to want?

It's embarrassing writing this, because I'm supposed to be the guy that has it together. But during this time, I tuned God out. When I got an email from one of her ex-fiances, Matt Damon—yeah, *Borne Identity* Matt Damon, I was even more in love, because Matt Damon was telling me how he missed out on an opportunity with her and how if I ever hurt her, he would come after me.

So, I shared this with my community group and a couple eye brows were raised, but they were happy for me. Until one of the guys in my group started telling me that she was lying. He didn't believe the Matt Damon stuff. There was no record of her working at Sony Records. She fed me lies and I believed them.

Why would she lie? I didn't want to believe it and didn't want to hear from anyone that she wasn't perfect. My mom couldn't stand her, my mentor family couldn't stand her, ummm when it came to those who thought she was great, I was standing in the severe minority.

I couldn't see straight, I was so in love. I remember walking into my apartment confused. Everyone seemed to be against her. My mom, my community group, the Brodersens—all thought I was nuts for even considering such a woman. But why?

Sure she was young in her faith and had bouts with lying, but she loved everyone. She was kind and generous with people. She was trying, and she shared her faith openly (at least that is what she told me). But deep down I knew something wasn't right. I went to my apartment buried my face into my couch and prayed.

"Dear God," I started, "please give me wisdom here. I know something isn't right, but I love this girl. I love her with every ounce of my being and I know it's crazy. Something inside me says there is something that isn't right. Every godly counsel You have ever given me does not support this, but I can't break it off with her if You don't speak to me clearly. I need You."

I prayed that over and over for what seemed to be an hour. I had frequented the First Baptist Prayer Tower in downtown Dallas many times waiting for God to respond. But the only thing I heard from God concerning her was "run." I decided that couldn't be God, because—well, I loved her, and that didn't sound very loving.

After praying I walked over to my laptop and typed her full name into Google. References to her being an actress popped up, but then there was a strange reference to her name and another guy. It listed her name next to a wedding date. My RPMs redlined as I clicked on the link. I saw her in a wedding gown. I didn't want to believe it. I saw her kissing another man. I saw her wedding cake with the date of a month ago. Everything inside me melted.

My thoughts spun. I kept walking to the couch and then picked up my phone to call her. I put the phone down. I texted her. It was over. I hit the floor in the fetal position and wept. My mom called, and I picked it up. She asked what was wrong. I tried to explain, but the emotion kept choking me. Within an hour my mom came and just held me like I was five and had just skinned my knee. Eventually the tears stopped and Mom went home. Moms just know how to be there.

I had never had my heart broken like that. I had never been hurt so deeply, but there was nothing I could do now. It was over. I walked over to the window and watched the naked trees wave. I cried to the Lord to take the pain. I prayed that this pain would not be for nothing—that somehow the Lord could use this.

I put in a *24* DVD and let Jack Bauer save the world for a straight 24 hours. My phone rang over and over again. I didn't want to talk to anyone. I didn't want to hear the words, "I told you so" I didn't want to die that painful death again and relive it. I just wanted to fast forward life.

Like Samson, God allowed me to go through that. Maybe that was even part of the plan. God got glory from it. I went running back to Him. His ways proved to be right. His love is always powerful and protective. It was a painful death for me that I hope to never relive. To be honest, I wish it never happened. I sinned greatly. If I was above it all, I would have not sinned against her. But fear of losing someone you think you're supposed to be with makes you do weird things. That fear creates weird ways of trying to keep holding on to this broken image of perfection.

God gave me Adrienne three years later. It felt like an infinitely long three years. But it happened, and I am so grateful for my wife. However, if I could go back, I would have listened to the Lord and to my community and to my family and walked away from Delilah.

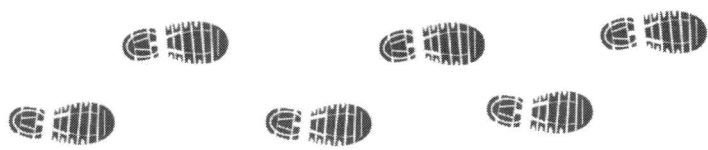

section five

PRESCRIPTIVE DATING

Learning from the triumphs and tragedies of warriors turns into doctrine. There is an art and a science to warfare. There are certain principles that are never violated. To violate them would put the soldier or those in his unit in danger.

Simple things from facing the correct side of the claymore toward the enemy to more complicated things such as conducting a joint raid, all have been mastered to a point that they now have doctrine. To not follow doctrine would put the lives of everyone in danger. However, where doctrine is silent the warrior is able to vary the art of war to meet his commander's intent.

However, to get to that point where the art of war was able to flourish, the warrior had to master the basics. Simple tasks such as firing a rifle, room clearing, and applying first aid must be mastered. Repetition, encouragement, and correction were the only ways to seal into the memory a warrior's way.

Eventually in my dancing career, I knew that making it up was only going to get me so far. My frustration with myself and my dance partner would only increase. So I caved and went to as many dance lessons as I could. Country, latin, ballroom, if it had a beat, I learned to dance to it. Sure the instructors were draconian in their prescription of dancing, but they were masters at the craft. That, of course, helped me figure out how to keep rhythm and that doing all the flashy stuff isn't so awesome if the woman looked like a sagging windsock.

Listening to them and learning their method helped me to understand the dance. Then I modified certain pieces of the dance that was more my style.

The dance when taught is simple. The feet eventually know where to go without thinking, but it takes practice and careful correction. In our culture we just throw our sons and daughters out there and sometimes mock and laugh as they flounder in the dating world.

Most fathers never explain to their sons what he is to value in a woman. Therefore the son will pick up those values from whoever is preaching them. Billboards, beer commercials, and the media have given men what it is they should value in a woman. It has come down to one thing: sex appeal.

Many men have grown up in this generation with fathers who, for the most part, have never been involved in the dating lives of their sons. But then again, who has ever been trained how to date?

There are marriage counselors who talk through the ins and outs of marriage. There are counselors to walk a person through how to get over a destructive habit, but when has the church ever had a dating counselor to help singles navigate the second biggest decision of their life?

These next several lessons are very direct in the type of man or woman someone should look for as well as how to go about dating them.

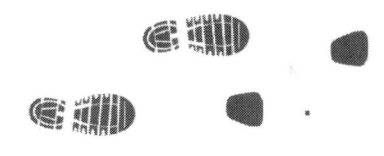

chapter fifteen:
THE SEARCH

God is in the process of partnering with you to find your future spouse. We all agree with that. We all agree that partnering with God's gift of parents and others that love you is a wise move.

Everyone has studied Proverbs 31, but for the most part, we do a "yeah, got it" to verses 1-9. Read a little about women knitting and the fact that they don't sleep and their kids and husband love them, then we highlight, verses 29 and 30,

> "Many women do noble things, but you surpass them all.
> Charm is deceptive, and beauty is fleeting; but a woman who fears the LORD is to be praised."

We buy our mom a coffee mug with that verse slapped on there for Mother's Day and then go back to trying to find a spouse desperately trying not to care about the way she looks.

I want to take a moment to bring some context back to this

scripture. In the first half of Proverbs 31 we find that the author was a woman: King Lemuel's mom. Jewish Tradition held that King Lemuel was actually Solomon and that King Lemuel's mother was Bathsheba. I have nothing to argue against it. I wouldn't bet my salvation on it, but I don't see Lemuel anywhere else in the scripture.

Proverbs 31:1-3 (ESV):

The words of King Lemuel. An oracle that his mother taught him:

What are you doing, my son? What are you doing, son of my womb? What are you doing, son of my vows? Do not give your strength to women, your ways to those who destroy kings.

Observation/Interpretation:

So here we have a concerned mother, Bathsheba, not exactly thrilled with her young son's choices in women. I think all of us have had a mom say something to that effect. That's what mom's do; they worry about their sons. They worry that the woman they marry will shipwreck them. They will turn their career to failure. Turn them from a married man to a three-time loser, who now has to move back home. Trust me, your mom has those thoughts.

The point she is making here is that a son dedicated to God has no business going after women that want him for his hefty bank account and life on easy street. Reality check for men: If you win her with your money, you will lose her with your lack of cash. Reality check for women: If you win him with your body, you will lose him when you lose the tightness on your tummy.

Proverbs 31:4-7 (ESV):

It is not for kings, O Lemuel, it is not for kings to drink wine, or for rulers to take strong drink, lest they drink and forget what has been decreed and pervert the rights of all the afflicted. Give strong drink to the one who is perishing, and wine to those in bitter distress; let them drink and forget their poverty and remember their misery no more.

Observation/Interpretation

Lemuel's mom then admonishes her son not to waste his life. Simple stuff here. Leave being an idiot to those on the streets. Some scholars argue that leaving the drinking and drugging to those who were poor and destitute is tongue in cheek. The point that Lemmy's mom is getting across is that classy men don't waste their lives like those who have no hope or future. In fact she goes on to teach him to be an example to them and look after those who are poor.

Proverbs 31:8-9 (ESV)
> Open your mouth for the mute, for the rights of all who are destitute. Open your mouth, judge righteously, defend the rights of the poor and needy.

Observation/Interpretation

King Lemuel was to be a truly noble man. He was to speak up for those who couldn't speak up for themselves. He would be a modern day social justice hero. Here was where Lemmy's mom made it very clear about the most important part of his life. She spent two verses telling him not to go after whores, three verses on not being an alcoholic or drug addict, two verses on looking out for the rights of others and ruling fairly, and then she spent 21 verses on finding the right woman. I guess it's kinda important.

Proverbs 31:10-12	
The Message	ESV
A good woman is hard to find, and worth far more than diamonds. Her husband trusts her without reserve, and never has reason to regret it. Never spiteful, she treats him generously all her life long.	[10] An excellent wife who can find? She is far more precious than jewels. [11] The heart of her husband trusts in her, and he will have no lack of gain. [12] She does him good, and not harm, all the days of her life.

Observation/Interpretation:

The first thing that King Lemuel's mother shared with her son was that a good woman was hard to find. This implied that finding a good woman wasn't going to be easy. It would take time. He would need the ability to discern a good woman from a not-so-good woman. It would be the most important investment he would ever make.

But the reality is a good woman is hard to find. Strange, 3000 years later, men are still nodding in agreement. The interesting thing is that men in that day were looking for the wrong kind of "good". Things haven't changed. She would go on to explain what good looks like, but for a moment she let him know that when he found a good woman he needed to hold on to her, because she was worth more than money could ever hope to buy.

The first characteristic of this good woman was that she didn't give her husband negativity. She treated him with unbelievable love and sought to do him good all his life. How many marriages do you know look like that? How many times have you seen a woman dotingly look at her husband and thinking to herself, "I wonder how I can do him good, today." In America, it seems that if a couple merely gets along, they are doing fantastic. But this woman does her man good, and not harm. She seeks to serve her husband.

APPLICATION

- Men, take time to search for a good woman. It's worth it.

- Men, find a woman who looks for opportunities to do good to those she loves.

- Women, be positive and seek opportunities to do good to others.

Proverbs 31:13-19	
Message	ESV
She shops around for the best yarns and cottons, and enjoys knitting and sewing. She's like a trading ship that sails to faraway places and brings back exotic surprises. She's up before dawn, preparing breakfast for her family and organizing her day. She looks over a field and buys it, then, with money she's put aside, plants a garden. First thing in the morning, she dresses for work, rolls up her sleeves, eager to get started. She senses the worth of her work, is in no hurry to call it quits for the day. She's skilled in the crafts of home and hearth, diligent in homemaking.	[13] She seeks wool and flax, and works with willing hands. [14] She is like the ships of the merchant; she brings her food from afar. [15] She rises while it is yet night and provides food for her household and portions for her maidens. [16] She considers a field and buys it; with the fruit of her hands she plants a vineyard. [17] She dresses herself with strength and makes her arms strong. [18] She perceives that her merchandise is profitable. Her lamp does not go out at night. [19] She puts her hands to the distaff, and her hands hold the spindle.

Observation/Interpretation:

This woman knew how to shop, where to shop, and a good deal when she saw one. She didn't have debt. She knew how to save money and invest it. She had no image or self-esteem issues. She understood the importance of who she was and what she did.

She worked until whatever needed to be done was done. Laziness was not in her vocabulary. She crafted her work with skill. She used the spindle and distaff with expertise. The "distaff" was a rod that held raw wool while spinning. The "spindle" was the stick the spinner twirled between her fingers that took up the spun wool.

This woman handled her money with wisdom. This is something that men could learn from as well. Financial stress is one of the leading causes of divorce. That doesn't mean we steal a bank roster and see who is doing well and then pick from that assortment, but it does mean that someone who handles their money well, generally handles their life well.

APPLICATION

- Men, look for a woman who knows how to dress for less.

   That isn't a plug for Ross, but it is a plug for a woman who knows how to put herself together without going into debt.

- Men, look for a woman with a solid self-image who values what she does.

   If a person doesn't value themselves, then they can't serve you out of a generous heart, but rather out of a heart that is constantly looking to you for worth. And when, not if, you make a mistake in the marriage—i.e. sin against her—you will find a deep struggle that will lead to other issues of lost trust.

- Men, look for a woman who loves what she does and isn't lazy.

- Ask questions about financial stability.

Proverbs 31:20-22	
Message	ESV
She's quick to assist anyone in need, reaches out to help the poor. She doesn't worry about her family when it snows; their winter clothes are all mended and ready to wear. She makes her own clothing, and dresses in colorful linens and silks.	She opens her hand to the poor and reaches out her hands to the needy.[21] She is not afraid of snow for her household, for all her household are clothed in scarlet. [22] She makes bed coverings for herself; her clothing is fine linen and purple.

Observations/Interpretations:

This woman served the poor, but never neglected the needs of her own family. In fact, her family was dressed to the nines. She didn't over spiritualize herself. She gave to the poor and helped those in need. However, she didn't put on rags herself or allow her family to not look their best. This woman didn't do ministry out of her own brokenness, but out of her love and generosity.

You are probably friends with at least one or two people who are socially off. They over-spiritualize what they do when they give to the poor, but you can't deny they are out there rain, sleet, or snow helping poor people. Then they remind you how unspiritual you are for not doing likewise. They may even criticize you for not shopping at the thrift store.

There are some people who are the really cool Bohemian types that shop at the thrift store and hang out with the poor and have that really chill, laid-back personality. I'm not talking about them. I'm talking about the person who is always finding some crisis with which they need to be involved. They are always talking about how little sleep they got. They are always talking about how little they actually got to eat. They are always sharing a story about some wayward person that they *had* to help. There is no joy there. They are merely covering up their brokenness and not dealing with their hurt. Instead of turning to drugs, alcohol, or some other coping mechanism, they have chosen to find someone worse-off than themselves to dive into and share in his or her misery.

I think that is better than drugs or alcohol, but it doesn't solve the real issue. The person needs to turn their issues over to Jesus by dealing with their struggles in community.

APPLICATION

- Men, find a woman who reaches out to the poor.

- Men, find a woman who knows how to take care of themselves and those she loves.

- Avoid daters who do ministry out of a coping mechanism.

Proverbs 31:23	
Message	ESV
Her husband is greatly respected when he deliberates with the city fathers.	Her husband is known in the gates when he sits among the elders of the land.

Observation/Interpretation:

This woman knew how to pick a man (or had great parents who could orchestrate a marriage). She got a man respected by the leaders of the community. What a huge deal that was. On the flip-side, her character was one that brought nothing but praise upon her husband. She was looking out for and looking to advance his career.

So, ladies, the question has to be asked of the guy you're dating or wanting to date. Does he have the respect of the leaders of your community? And, men, does she have the capacity to help you in your career? If she is not into your career, you will have a huge divide. How many hours a day will you spend on doing your career? Let's say a minimum of 40 hours a week. That is how food gets on the table. That's how the bills are paid, and that is where a huge part of your joy in life *should* be found.

If she is not interested in what you do, it's hard for her to support what you do and help you advance. Ladies, if you want to win a man, encourage him in his career. He needs to know that you are going to be behind him in whatever he does.

APPLICATION

- Women, find a man respected by the leaders of your community.

- Men, find a woman who selflessly helps others succeed.

Proverbs 31:24-27	
Message	ESV
She designs gowns and sells them, brings the sweaters she knits to the dress shops. Her clothes are well-made and elegant, and she always faces tomorrow with a smile. When she speaks she has something worthwhile to say, and she always says it kindly. She keeps an eye on everyone in her household, and keeps them all busy and productive.	She makes linen garments and sells them; she delivers sashes to the merchant. [25] Strength and dignity are her clothing, and she laughs at the time to come. [26] She opens her mouth with wisdom, and the teaching of kindness is on her tongue. [27] She looks well to the ways of her household and does not eat the bread of idleness.

Observation/Interpretation:

This woman knew how to run a home. No laziness here. She was busy, and her house was organized and everyone knew their role. But oddly enough, she was not a tyrant. Kindness dripped off her lips. It's one thing to work hard. It's another thing altogether to work hard and be kind. She doesn't sweat the small things and looks to serve rather than be served. She also looked good in the midst of her work. But then it's hard not to be attractive when you are so kind and warm.

Men, I want you to notice it's this woman's kindness and industrious nature which make her even more attractive. That is what you're looking for.

APPLICATION

- Find a woman who is not lazy.

- Find a woman who can run a house.

- Find a woman who is kind.

Proverbs 31:28-29	
Message	ESV
Her children respect and bless her; her husband joins in with words of praise: "Many women have done wonderful things, but you've outclassed them all!"	[28] Her children rise up and call her blessed; her husband also, and he praises her: [29] "Many women have done excellently, but you surpass them all."

Observation/Interpretation:

Everyone reading this desires their family to say this of them. That kind of praise doesn't come undeserved. This woman had outdone them all. She had worked hard and had received the praise she deserved. Her husband knew that she needed to be recognized and did so accordingly. He didn't try and steal the spotlight when it was her turn to be recognized. He wanted to lift her up and that might be the reason she worked so hard, she was loved well.

Notice that you didn't hear her rejecting praise in some sort of false humility. She just accepted it. She didnn't over-spiritualize it and talk about how she was just God's servant and that it was really nothing. She just accepted it.

APPLICATION

- Women, find a man who knows how to affirm others.

- Men, find a woman who knows how to take a compliment.

- Look for a partner who knows how to share the "spotlight."

Proverbs 31:30-31	
Message	ESV
Charm can mislead and beauty soon fades. The woman to be admired and praised is the woman who lives in the Fear-of-GOD. Give her everything she deserves! Festoon her life with praises!	Charm is deceitful, and beauty is vain, but a woman who fears the LORD is to be praised. [31] Give her of the fruit of her hands, and let her works praise her in the gates.

Observation/Interpretation:

Here are the verses that we all know. We must take them in context with what has preceded it. The woman that King Lemuel's mom described might as well be the CEO of a Fortune 500 company. The reason she received praise wasn't her looks or charm.

A lot of women needing attention use every flirt trick in the book to get it. I'm not talking about women who are fun or nice. I'm talking about the ones that paw every man they come in contact with and fish for compliments. Unchecked charm will mislead other men to think she is really interested in them. I promise you it never bodes well for those who search after shiny things.

The woman that King Lemuel's mother wanted for her son was one that lived in the Fear-of-God. She didn't live for her husband. She lived for God. Men, you want that every time. She won't be affected when you're an idiot. She doesn't serve you, because of how magnanimous and wonderful you are, but because she fears the Lord.

The great thing about being this kind of woman is that it results in reward from her family and the community. People want to be around her. She doesn't search out praise, but you can't help but praise her.

APPLICATION

- Men, stop searching for the Mother Teresa who is also a Victoria's Secret model.

- Men, find a woman who lives in the fear of God.

- Women, live in the fear of God.

Ladies, I am serious here. If you live in the fear of being single, get ready for your worst nightmare. If you live in the fear of I-don't-want-to-break-up-with-him-cause-it-might-hurt, then you are walking into a catastrophe. Whether you are afraid of it hurting him or it hurting you, be wise and end it. In the end, he'll thank you for letting him get on with his life.

chapter sixteen:
MUST BE A BELIEVER

I'm not sure if 2nd Corinthians 6:14 is on a coffee cup, but it is quoted so often I have to think it is somewhere: refrigerator magnet, coffee cup, bumper sticker...something.

> Do not be yoked together with unbelievers. For what do righteousness and wickedness have in common? Or what fellowship can light have with darkness?

This verse has been used out of context probably since the Corinthians received the letter back in 56 A.D. The good thing is that even though it's used out of context, the main idea is still correct and should be followed. Don't marry an unbeliever.

However, just so you know, this wasn't what Paul was talking about at all in his letter. He wanted to make things right between him and the Corinthians. Some in the church had disputed his apostleship and authority. They questioned his integrity because he changed his travel plans and hadn't visited when he said he would.

So Paul wrote 2 Corinthians to let them know that he forgave them, and anyone they forgave, he forgave. So in this portion of scripture he is referencing those who had strong ties to non-believers which led them to sin. Paul was never against interacting with non-believers, because then you would have to leave the world. I'm not sure if you noticed, but heathens are everywhere. What Paul was against was joining them in their sin.

2 Corinthians 6:11-13 (ESV)
    We have spoken freely to you, Corinthians; our heart is wide open. You are not restricted by us, but you are restricted in your own affections. In return (I speak as to children) widen your hearts also.

In these three verses, he is speaking as a father to disciplined children. He wanted them not to be hurt by the potency of his discipline, but rather see his heart and his love for them. He is asking them to open their hearts and to love him again. He then is going to show them through their actions how they can show their love.

2 Corinthians 6:14 (ESV)
    Do not be unequally yoked with unbelievers. For what partnership has righteousness with lawlessness? Or what fellowship has light with darkness?

Observation/Interpretation:
    Ok, this is simple. Paul didn't want the believers to be yoked to the darkness of non-believers. This applied in all areas of life. He didn't want any Christian to be connected to a non-believer that caused them to go down a path of sin. I know I'm going to ruffle feathers when I say this, but there isn't a qualifier for how Christian someone is.

You can't just assume that the guy you're checking out is a believer because he wrote *Christian,* on his Facebook profile or Match.com.

At the same time there isn't a qualifier for what marks a person and his spirituality. The term "yoked" is a farming term. When two oxen are pulling a plow, they are yoked together by a huge heavy unbreakable wooden thing. Paul wanted believers to connect themselves to those going the right direction—towards Christ and not towards idolatry.

2 Corinthians 6:15-16 (ESV)

> What accord has Christ with Belial? Or what portion does a believer share with an unbeliever? What agreement has the temple of God with idols? For we are the temple of the living God; as God said, "I will make my dwelling among them and walk among them, and I will be their God, and they shall be my people.

Observation/Interpretation:

Paul asked three rhetorical questions that related to the combination of a believer and a non-believer to a pact Jesus made with Satan. Belial in this age was another name for the Devil. The temple of God referred to the Jerusalem temple and the fact no one would ever dream of putting foreign idols in there. Because we have the Holy Spirit, we are now the temple of the living God. Paul quoted the Old Testament here. Paul could have referred any number of verses in the Bible with that statement, but most likely one of these four (or all) were in his head.

Exodus 29:45 (ESV)	Leviticus 26:12 (ESV)	Jeremiah 31:1 (ESV)	Ezekiel 37:27 (ESV)
I will dwell among the people of Israel and will be their God.	And I will walk among you and will be your God, and you shall be my people.	"At that time, declares the LORD, I will be the God of all the clans of Israel, and they shall be my people."	My dwelling place shall be with them, and I will be their God, and they shall be my people.

So just as in the times of the Old Testament when God physically lived among the people in the tabernacle, now God lives inside all believers. That is why Paul stressed living in a way that honored God.

2 Corinthians 6:17-18 (ESV)
> Therefore go out from their midst, and be separate from them, says the Lord, and touch no unclean thing; then I will welcome you, and I will be a father to you, and you shall be sons and daughters to me, says the Lord Almighty."

Observation/Interpretation:

Yikes! Go out from their midst? Does that mean only go to the Christian coffee shops, gyms, and mechanics? Is the Shepherd's Guide our only source for doing business with anyone? No. Paul is saying that Christians should be in the world, but not of the world. He quoted Isaiah 52:11.

In Isaiah 52, God called his people to leave Babylon and its idolatrous ways. He then applied the idolatry experienced by His people with Babylon to how these Corinthian Christians involved themselves in pagan idolatry through their compromise of their spiritual lives.

APPLICATION

- Only marry a believer.

chapter seventeen:
HOW

There are a million dating books out there telling you how to date. If we are honest, they are more of good ideas by good Christian men and women as opposed to God's word. The problem we as Christian advisors, counselors, and friends face is that anyone can get married. In fact, dating in general is a small stint of life that preceeds a very long stint of life. We spend so much time worrying about it, because we have made our wedding day comparable to the Super Bowl.

I know couples that were barely Christian. They were sleeping with each other, partying, not exactly faithful, and somehow now they have an awesome marriage. I know others that dated and were incredibly pure and did everything "right" and are now divorced. So just because you date well doesn't guarantee anything. God's mercy is what we are all desperately dependent on, and until you get that, nothing else really matters.

The Bible doesn't give specific advice for dating couples, but I pulled several verses that I felt in context apply to those of us trying to figure out how to go about this thing of finding a life partner. Following these verses guarantees you nothing, other than you will be following God's moral will. It doesn't mean you will get married.

If I just had one piece of advice for those dating and I knew that everything else would be ignored, I would say this: stay pure. I know that may seem too simple, but that is the only thing you have to do. You are free to go after any Christian single you want as long as you keep it pure.

1 Corinthians 6:18-20

Before Paul gave his thoughts on singleness and marriage in 1 Corinthians 7, he addressed some matters in the church that disturbed him. One of them was some serious sexual immorality that would make the heathens at the strip club blush. Paul hit it head on and essentially chided the Corinthians for their obsession with sex. The Corinthians were known for being surrounded by sin. In that day, to go on a debaucherous weekend with the boys was also known as "playing the Corinthian."

So Paul explained that sex was something that was good, but it wasn't ultimate. When anything other than the Lord becomes the object of our obsessions and affections, we have idolatry.

1 Corinthians 6:13-14 (ESV)
> "Food is meant for the stomach and the stomach for food"—and God will destroy both one and the other. The body is not meant for sexual immorality, but for the Lord, and the Lord for the body. And God raised the Lord and will also raise us up by his power.

Observation/Interpretation:
God created the human body with one purpose in mind: to glorify Himself.

The stomach can't process rocks. It processes food. Anything else causes it to shut down and stop working. The same truth applies for our body. It was made for one thing. It was made to house the Lord. Sexual immorality causes a breakdown between body and spirit.

Paul added one line in verse 14. He made the claim that the same power that raised Jesus from the dead will raise those who believe in Him from the dead. He then transitioned with a reminder of eternal things.

1 Corinthians 15-17 (ESV)
> Do you not know that your bodies are members of Christ? Shall I then take the members of Christ and make them members of a prostitute? Never! Or do you not know that he who is joined to a prostitute becomes one body with her? For, as it is written, "The two will become one flesh."
> But he who is joined to the Lord becomes one spirit with him.

Observation/Interpretation:
Paul jumped back to Genesis for God's intention for sex. God utilized a physical act to represent a spiritual and emotional reality. No one would ever want to experience spiritual and emotional oneness with a prostitute. But that is how the Lord is affected by our sin.

He compared the act of sexual union and the oneness experienced in marriage to the oneness that God experiences with the believer. It's not a sexual oneness, but rather a complete spiritual oneness.

There is a oneness between a husband and wife that should not be connected to any other person. In the same way, God and the believer experience a oneness that should not be connected with any other idol, especially sex.

1 Corinthians 6:18-20 (NIV)
> Flee from sexual immorality. Every other sin a person commits is outside the body, but the sexually immoral person sins against his own body. Or do you not know that your body is a temple of the Holy Spirit within you, whom you have from God? You are not your own, for you were bought

with a price. So glorify God in your body.

Observation/Interpretation:

Flee, escape, run. Don't try and test your spiritual will. You will lose. I had a buddy of mine in the army who once tried to test his spiritual will-power by seeing if he or his female friend would break first into immorality. Yeah, bizarre.

APPLICATION

- Glorify God in your body by fleeing from sexual immorality.

- Create a plan for purity

See Appendix: How for a real life illustration

1 Timothy 5:1-2

In Paul's first epistle to Timothy, he wrote to encourage the young leader on how to handle the people in his church. He had some particularly tough tasks as most of the people in the congregation were older and looked at Timothy like everyone looks at the youth pastor. Nice, but having no authority over the lives of real people—parents. Yet, Paul encouraged Timothy to live above the stereotype. In verses one and two of chapter 5, Paul wasn't necessarily talking about dating here, but it applies: 1 Timothy 5:2 is very clear about how we are to approach the opposite sex.

1 Timothy 5:1-2 (NIV)
    Treat younger men as brothers, older women as mothers,
    and younger women as sisters, with absolute purity.

I love the NIV's rendering off the word $\pi\alpha\sigma\eta$, which means all, but has a deeper meaning of complete or absolute. We can derive Paul meant sexual purity, but does purity mean anything beyond that? This takes the guess work of how to treat one another. Treating a woman you are/might be/could be/ there's a chance/interested in is simply treating her like your sister. This flies in the face of many guys who say things like, "She's like my sister! I could never date her."

On the contrary, that is the one you could date. I know we are in semantics here and the reality most likely is that you are not interested in the girl who reminds you of your sister. I get that, but let's not say, she's like my sister—say, "I'm just not that into you."

1 Thessalonians 4:1-8

This command is directed at men, but has relevance the other way around. Paul wrote in a direct manner to express what God's will was for the Thessalonians. You've probably asked this a million times. "What is God's Will for my life?" Well, here it is.

1 Thessalonians 4:1-8 (ESV)
Finally, then, brothers, we ask and urge you in the Lord Jesus, that as you received from us how you ought to walk and to please God, just as you are doing, that you do so more and more. For you know what instructions we gave you through the Lord Jesus.

For this is the will of God, your sanctification: that you abstain from sexual immorality; that each one of you know how to control his own body in holiness and honor, not in the passion of lust like the Gentiles who do not know God; that no one transgress and wrong his brother in this matter, because the Lord is an avenger in all these things, as we told you beforehand and solemnly warned you.

For God has not called us for impurity, but in holiness. Therefore whoever disregards this, disregards not man but God, who gives his Holy Spirit to you.

Purity is not just kind of a big deal. It's a huge deal. Every time you turn the page in the Bible, Paul or some apostle is going off on purity. You already know how bad it hurts to cross the line physically and then not be married to the person.

Guilt.

Shame.

These are the things that Jesus went to the cross for and separates you from God, even though as a believer, God doesn't hold your sins against you. When you aren't physically pure, you are not growing in your relationship with God which is the ultimate goal of all relationships—that they draw you closer to God.

You already knew that. But there aren't just one or two verses that talk about purity. There are a slew that that pound the idea home.

Purity (or lack thereof) is what ruined your last relationship. That's why she was "psycho." That's why he wouldn't commit and treated you terribly. I know you don't believe me. I know you think I'm over doing the purity deal. Trust me, I've walked down the wrong road. It is that simple. That is why every other dating book in the world imposes odd things like "mandatory group dating." The reason it felt legalistic is because you didn't know the heart behind it. It was to protect you from yourself.

You have got to remember that after you get married, the forbiddeness of sex is gone. When was the last time you remember a steamy sex scene in a movie with two married people? It just doesn't happen, because that's not what is enticing. Enticing is almost getting caught. Enticing is dangerous. The girl that you only deal with for a night is way sexier than the girl who you walk in on in the midst of going "number 2."

APPLICATION

- Get with community to develop a plan to honor God in your dating life

Romans 13:12-14

A couple verses that speak to the heart of purity that I want you to embrace are Romans 13:12-14. Paul taught the Romans how to interact with one another and not take advantage of each other. This wasn't primarily a sexual pep talk, but rather an exhortation to not take advantage of one another—to be at peace with everyone as long

as it was up to you. He turned the corner and listed off all of the of-
fenses one can commit against another.

Romans 13:8-11(NASV)

Owe nothing to anyone except to love one another; for he
who loves his neighbor has fulfilled the law. For this, "You
shall not commit adultery, You shall not murder, you shall
not steal, you shall not covet," and if there is any other com-
mandment, it is summed up in this saying, "You shall love
your neighbor as yourself."

Love does no wrong to a neighbor; therefore love is the
fulfillment of the law. Do this, knowing the time, that it is
already the hour for you to awaken from sleep; for now salvation is nearer to us than when we believed.

The night is almost gone, and the day is near. Therefore
let us lay aside the deeds of darkness and put on the armor
of light.

Observation/Interpretation:

Paul spoke truth to an oversexed, over-stimulated community that
life wasn't about them. The Romans were to live life for one another. Not for themselves. Because we are reading this from a sexual
purity bias, we tend to think Paul was focused on sex.

This wasn't about sex. This was about how to live in peace with
one another. Don't take advantage of one another. In the quest for
our life-mate, we may feel that it is right to cross boundaries God
ordained, because "we love one another." That's not love, friends.
That's lust.

Romans 13:12-14 (NASV)

The night is almost gone, and the day is near. Therefore let
us lay aside the deeds of darkness and put on the armor of
light. Let us behave properly as in the day, not in carousing
and drunkenness, not in sexual promiscuity and sensuality,
not in strife and jealousy. But put on the Lord Jesus Christ,
and make no provision for the flesh in regard to its lusts.

Observation/Interpretation:

The truth is that everyone seems to be making a lot of provision for the flesh. What happened?

We have found that the outcome of crossing physical boundaries ends with terrible consequences. The couple feels intense guilt, shame, and embarrassment. Or the couple justifies their actions as a one-time occurrence. Then they run through a series of one-time occurrences.

Sex before marriage is no longer just for the drunk party kids, but a reality among the good youth group kids, camp counselors, and spiritual leaders.

The shame is that this is a *hidden* reality. The couple can never seem to confess their sin. Either they find themselves married one day or in many other identical relationships throughout college and young adult life.

For right now, I want you to pause, reflect, and memorize Romans 13:14 in your favorite version. This might be seem like a trite exercise, but my heart for you is that the Word of God might speak to you before you get into a situation, that later you will regret. I've given you four versions. Choose one and hide it in your heart.

APPLICATION

- Memorize Romans 13:14

Romans 13:14			
NASV	ESV	NET	NIV
But put on the Lord Jesus Christ, and make no provision for the flesh in regard to *its* lusts.	But put on the Lord Jesus Christ, and make no provision for the flesh, to gratify its desires.	Instead, put on the Lord Jesus Christ, and make no provision for the flesh to arouse its desires.	Rather, clothe yourselves with the Lord Jesus Christ, and do not think about how to gratify the desires of the sinful nature.

chapter eighteen:
GIVE ME STEPS

As I was getting ready to publish this book, I found myself sitting at a conference table with ten other men. We were trying to help our friend get over a relationship. The hurt from the break-up was so devastating that at one point he had called me from a sewer culvert. He had a gun to his head, and was ready to end his life. I conferenced in a friend of mine, JP. Since I was at Purdue University speaking to students, I couldn't go and get him. Thankfully, we talked him into giving us his location. He surrendered his gun to JP and now we still have my friend.

However, this hasn't changed the fact that his rejection is still real and now we have to put the training wheels back on to train him how to date. Theory is not going to help him. Bible verses provide only temporary comfort without tangible steps on what to do. So as we were sitting in the conference room we had to come up with a plan for our friend to retrain him how to guard his heart and how to date.

We first wanted to lay out that there were some spiritual issues going on. I think think that this will be helpful for you as well. You may not be suicidal, but you know as well as I do, you need help.

Romans 12:1-2 (ESV)

> I appeal to you therefore, brothers, by the mercies of God, to present your bodies as a living sacrifice, holy and acceptable to God, which is your spiritual worship. Do not be conformed to this world, but be transformed by the renewal of your mind, that by testing you may discern what is the will of God, what is good and acceptable and perfect.

Everyone wants to know God's will. We want to know who to marry, what job to get, and how He wants us to live our life. However, we are so clouded by our own sin and our own hearts that we can't figure any of that out. Paul taught that for us to be able to discern the will of God, we must have our minds renewed.

He is speaking to Christians here, so this isn't about simply accepting that Jesus died on the cross for your sins, and that he rose from the dead, so that you may receive the Holy Spirit.

This is different. To be able to discern what God is doing in and around us, we must be in tune with him. Our minds be focused on Him and His agenda. However, when we conform to the world, it's very difficult to make Christ our focus.

He called believers to be living sacrifices. To sacrifice what we want in order to gain a renewed mind. It's one thing to die for Christ, quite another to live for Him. We must remember that Holiness is what God is after. He wants His followers to have a marked difference from the world while still being an example in the world.

For some of us, we put behind our upbringing in how we treated the opposite sex and we renew our mind into a completely new culture. We had to do this for our friend who confessed Christ as savior, but found heartbreak leading him to the edge of despair. He needed his mind renewed. We gave him a plan. You might follow this plan or vary it according to your situation.

1. Guard your heart

We clarified what we meant by guarding the heart. Guarding your heart is from Proverbs 4 where Solomon warned his son not to travel in darkness. He admonished him to be holy and to hang out with the right people. He used the phrase in this context. "Guard your heart" meant, "Don't let evil get in your heart."

Proverb 4:20-27 (NIV)

My son, pay attention to what I say; listen closely to my words. Do not let them out of your sight, keep them within your heart; for they are life to those who find them and health to a man's whole body. Above all else, guard your heart, for it is the wellspring of life.

Put away perversity from your mouth; keep corrupt talk far from your lips. Let your eyes look straight ahead, fix your gaze directly before you. Make level paths for your feet and take only ways that are firm. Do not swerve to the right or the left; keep your foot from evil.

Notice the first half of Solomon's advice for his son is how he protected himself, and the second is how he should act out what he internalized. If a man kept his father's instruction in front of him all of his life, then he would be healthy, granted the father's advice was sound. Good thing for us is that although Solomon was flawed, our Heavenly Father is perfect. If we keep his words tucked neatly in our hearts, we will have awesome emotional health.

Evidence of someone being healthy on the inside is the way they control themselves on the outside. If corrupt talk comes out of their mouth, then it reveals what is already in the heart. That is not just for dirty locker room jokes, but for how we share sensitive information. So we decided that my friend would share all sensitive information with us. We would not allow Ralph to be tempted to share sensitive information that might emotionally bond him to a non-safe person (i.e. girl he finds attractive) for this season of life.

2. Community over Isolation

We communicated with Ralph that when he bought his house, picked his college, and picked his career that he had done things seeking out wise counsel. In some instances, he had been able to counsel some of us on the best way to handle money. He had a plan.

However, when it came to relationships, his engineering degree, financial responsibility, and personal disciplines weren't enough. He needed community.

Proverbs 15:22 (ESV)
> Plans fail for lack of counsel, but with many advisers they
> succeed.

3. Being a Burden

We asked Ralph if he thought we had the best of intentions laid out for him, and if he would trust us with his decision making in the area of his weakness. He said he would. The hardest thing for Ralph to do was be a burden. He was a model of self-sufficiency. Everything he did exuded competence. However, he found himself in despair when it came to relationships.

So we asked him to communicate with us regularly for simple decisions. He needed to practice being a burden. This might sound draconian, but the reason for this practice was not so we would control Ralph's life, but rather that our friend would let himself be out of control in the area of his life that brought him pain.

Isn't that why most of us won't bring others into our sin struggles? We don't really believe that they care. We think that after we share our hang ups, they will shrug their shoulders clueless and move on. We may not trust them for fear of them taking some legalistic measure to make our lives more miserable. For those struggling in sin, putting anything before God, they must practice accountability and learn when they can trust themselves.

Galatians 6:1-2 (NIV)
> Brothers and sisters, if someone is caught in a sin, you
> who live by the Spirit should restore that person gently. But
> watch yourselves, or you also may be tempted. Carry each

other's burdens, and in this way you will fulfill the law of Christ.

To implement this, we simply created a group text for everyone in our group to reply. When our friend had a decision to make, he simply asked the group. Now it wasn't like he had a relationship issue every day, but we knew that he wouldn't share decisions with us if he wasn't used to sharing decisions with us. So we started with things that were sort of ridiculous and kind of funny.

Like, "Hey guys, is it okay for me to skip this regeneration class for a therapy session?"

All of us gave a hearty thumbs-up. Our self-sufficient friend was learning how to be a burden. We found it impractical for ten of us to try and give insight into his life. So we trimmed the number down to three of us that would check in with Ralph daily.

4. Confession

Ralph told us that whenever he did something he knew to be inappropriate, that action would put him in a position of endangering his heart. He usually knew he shouldn't do it, but did it anyway. We told him that for us to help him, he needed to have accountability and confess to us whenever he put a want of relationship over a place of getting emotionally stable.

For Ralph, confessing hanging out with a woman and getting emotionally tied to her was his sin struggle. Another person might struggle with crossing physical boundaries with a girlfriend. Another might struggle with starving herself to look a certain way to get a guy. Confession is a healthy part of the Christian life. A proper practice of confession helps kill off our capacity to sin. Remember, we're not looking to moderate sin, we are looking to mortify sin.

James 5:13-16 (ESV)

    Is anyone among you suffering? Let him pray. Is anyone cheerful? Let him sing praise. Is anyone among you sick? Let him call for the elders of the church, and let them pray over him, anointing him with oil in the name of the Lord. And the prayer of faith will save the one who is sick, and the Lord will raise him up. And if he has committed sins, he will be forgiven. Therefore, confess your sins to one another and pray for one another, that you may be healed. The prayer of a righteous person has great power as it is working.

Observation/Interpretation:

James spoke to believers about the power of prayer. He knew that some had become sick because of sin. He knew that confession was a healthy part of being a Christian. If anyone was suffering or sick, he was to call on the elders to pray over him. Our friend gave us authority to be elders in his life. He committed to confess when he called his ex-girlfriend. He committed to confess when he had a physical rendezvous with a female friend. Confession is good for the soul and leads to healing.

5. Repentance

Confession without repentance is not helpful. Repentance is what will bring life to a person and peace to the soul. Jesus taught that repentance was the end goal for sinners. One time Jesus was at a party with sinners and the religious people started asking hard questions like "Why does Jesus hang out with sinners?" Jesus answer was pretty provocative.

Luke 5:31-32 (NIV)
Jesus answered them, "It is not the healthy who need a doctor, but the sick. I have not come to call the righteous, but sinners to repentance."

Observation/Interpretation:
Jesus accepts us when we are sick, but he doesn't want us to stay that way. He is always looking to bring sinners to repentance. The job of the group that Ralph had entrusted his life to was to make sure that after he confessed a sin, he didn't go out and just do the same thing again. We wanted him healthy. We didn't want him hurting. He needed us.

So the question to ask yourself is, how much do you trust you? If you've been in and out of relationships and would have no problem calling yourself an idiot for the ways of your past relationships, then perhaps you don't have a graduate degree in dating and need to turn the reigns of relationships over to someone else. Perhaps, creating a community for authenticity to help you make decisions for dating is all that you need. You know where you are. The main concern is that you recognize the degree to which you struggle and find appropriate accountability.

Even the Apostle Paul struggled with some areas of life. I don't know if it was dating, but I've echoed these words with Paul.

Romans 7:15-31 (ESV)
> For I do not understand my own actions. For I do not do what I want, but I do the very thing I hate...So I find it to be a law that when I want to do right, evil lies close at hand. For I delight in the law of God, in my inner being, but I see in my members another law waging war against the law of my mind and making me captive to the law of sin that dwells in my members. Wretched man that I am! Who will deliver me from this body of death? Thanks be to God through Jesus Christ our Lord! So then, I myself serve the law of God with my mind, but with my flesh I serve the law of sin.

If Paul needed help, I need help. You need help. We all need freedom from this body of death that is constantly taking us back to our old ways.

Here is the question. When will you surrender your way that hasn't worked for God's way that always will. What are you afraid of? What makes you afraid?

See Appendix: Give Me Steps for a real life illustration

APPLICATION

- Guard your heart. Practive emotional and physical boundaries.

- Seek community over isolation. Community prevents bad decisions.

- Allow yourself to be a burden to others.

- Practice regular confession. That means drawing personal boundaries for yourself that may not be sinful, but give you enough margin so that you don't always find yourself tightroping sin.

- Practice regular repentance.

chapter nineteen:

DATING THE DIVORCED

In America, divorce is common. However, talking about dating for the divorced is a bit uncomfortable. So for those who are divorced and want to date or for those thinking of dating someone divorced, we wanted to draw the truth for us from scripture.

God hates divorce. Hates it. In Malachi, God railed the Jews for their inability to rid themselves of Babylon's idolatrous practices. He also hit them hard on their lack of looking after the needs of others. In fact, some divorced their wives because they couldn't have children. They complained to God that they had fallen on hard times, and God had not given them justice. In this last book of the Old Testament, Malachi confronted them on their sin and called them to repentance.

We pick up verse fourteen in the midst of God confronting the Jews on their marital infidelity.

Malachi 2:14-15 (ESV)

"...the LORD was witness between you and the wife of your youth, to whom you have been faithless, though she is your companion and your wife by covenant. Did he not make them one, with a portion of the Spirit in their union? And what was the one God seeking? Godly offspring. So guard yourselves in your spirit, and let none of you be faithless to the wife of your youth."

Observation/Interpretation:

God was at the wedding. He was present at the ceremony as a witness to the covenant that the man and woman made. God made them one person for the purpose of giving the Lord godly offspring. The men were divorcing their wives and ruining families.

Verse 16 is how God felt about it.

Malachi 2:16	
ESV	NASV
[16] "For the man who does not love his wife but divorces her, says the LORD, the God of Israel, covers his garment with violence, says the LORD of hosts.	[16] "For I hate divorce," says the LORD, the God of Israel, "and him who covers his garment with wrong," says the LORD of hosts.

Observation/Interpretation:

Most translations go with the latter of "I hate divorce." But the more literal reading is the ESV here. The main point is that God thinks divorce is bad. God doesn't hate divorced people. He hates divorce because it hurts the very ones he loves. Within the context of this time period, the men were divorcing their wives for the hot foreigner non-believers. God let them know exactly what he thought of that.

APPLICATION

- Reconciliation is the first best option for a broken marriage

Is the divorced person now only in God's will if they are forever single? I want to explore that in detail for both sides of the coin: from the never married single looking at dating a divorced person to the divorced person looking to date again.

In some instances the Bible is clear. In other situations we are left to evaluate the circumstances using biblical principles.

First off, we must remember that as followers of Jesus Christ, we have been called to a "ministry of reconciliation" calling all people to be reconciled to God. Though consistently unfaithful to our creator, our Bride Groom, He has faithfully pursued all people that they might be reconciled to Him. As those who have been reconciled, believers have been given this message and this ministry to call unfaithful lovers back to reconciliation with God.

A divorced believer has a unique ministry with their former spouse and should view the issue of remarriage in light of this higher calling.

Okay with that said, let me try and give some principles to follow.

> If the former spouse is dead, then remarriage is allowed.

> The remarriage of one's divorced spouse may be viewed as severing the former marriage so that the unmarried spouse may be free to remarry a believer. You could call that infidelity if you needed a more biblical word and clearly Jesus was okay with divorce in this case. (People are free to disagree with me here, but this is where I err on the side of grace for the divorced.)

Things get sticky when the former spouse has not remarried. The scriptures don't go there.

God gave essentially three provisions for divorce in His Word. In a sense, divorce is always the result of sin, but isn't necessarily always a sin. Here they are.

1. Adultery   2. Abandonment   3. Abuse

Adultery

In the case where there has been sexual immorality, we look at
Matthew 19:9 (NIV)

> Jesus said, "But I tell you that anyone who divorces his
> wife, except for marital unfaithfulness, causes her to become
> an adulteress, and anyone who marries the divorced woman
> commits adultery."

Observation/Interpretation

Jesus didn't mince words. If a person has sex outside of marriage,
that person becomes an adulterer. If your former spouse committed adultery against you then you are free to marry another. I think
Jesus put this provision into marriage, because of how difficult it is
to trust someone who has betrayed another at the most base level of
a relationship. God's heart on this is still reconciliation.

Jesus also warned his audience that a man should seek to marry
a woman whose husband divorced her. Anyone who married the
woman didn't have proper grounds for divorce and sinned against
God.

APPLICATION

- For the one who committed adultery. If you cannot
  reconcile with your spouse, you should not remarry until
  your spouse has remarried or severed the relationship
  through their own infidelity.

- Jesus permits remarriage for those who have been cheat-
  ed on.

- Do not date a person who is in a marriage that still has
  the possibility of being reconciled.

- Do not date a divorced person who still has a chance of
  reconciling that marriage.

Abandonment

In the case where an unbelieving spouse leaves a believing spouse, we look at 1 Corinthians 7:12-16. The important thing to remember was that Paul was trying to keep Christian marriages together. He came across a topic that the Lord had never taught on during his earthly ministry. He gave the situation of divorcing an unbeliever all the wisdom that he had.

1 Corinthians 7:12-17 (ESV)

...if any brother has a wife who is an unbeliever, and she consents to live with him, he should not divorce her. If any woman has a husband who is an unbeliever, and he consents to live with her, she should not divorce him.

For the unbelieving husband is made holy because of his wife, and the unbelieving wife is made holy because of her husband. Otherwise your children would be unclean, but as it is, they are holy.

But if the unbelieving partner separates, let it be so. In such cases the brother or sister is not enslaved. God has called you to peace.

For how do you know, wife, whether you will save your husband? Or how do you know, husband, whether you will save your wife?

Only let each person lead the life that the Lord has assigned to him, and to which God has called him. This is my rule in all the churches.

Observation/Interpretation:

The term "made holy" is what we would see as sanctify or to set apart for God. So both the unbelieving spouse and the children of a mixed home are set apart when the marriage is together. This doesn't mean they are better off than a Christian home, but rather that God has special grace for those operating in this environment.

God gave Paul, a single guy, a tender perspective on a relational dynamic to which he wasn't personally privy. He understood relational dynamics to a point where he could say confidently that if the unbelieving spouse leaves, let him. He was looking for peace in the home and not discord and that would be a definite cause of discord. We also have to remember that this isn't Paul's opinion, but rather inspired by God. The goal for each believer was to follow the plan God had given him.

APPLICATION

- If your unbelieving spouse divorces you, the Bible says you are free to marry another.

- Look to reconcile with an unbelieving spouse who is willing to stay in the marriage.

Abuse

Now let's get real. Abuse happens in marriages. Physical, verbal, emotional, and sexual abuse is real and impacts spouses and children. This is where we get antsy. The Bible doesn't directly address this.

Matthew 18:15-17 (ESV)
> "If your brother sins against you, go and tell him his fault, between you and him alone. If he listens to you, you have gained your brother. But if he does not listen, take one or two others along with you, that every charge may be established by the evidence of two or three witnesses.
>
> If he refuses to listen to them, tell it to the church. And if he refuses to listen even to the church, let him be to you as a Gentile and a tax collector.

Observation/Interpretation:

So in terms of sin between spouses, first the abused spouse must confront the abuse with their sinning mate. If the spouse repents then marital healing can begin. If not, the abused spouse brings in one or two others from their Christian community to reconcile in an attempt to help the abusing spouse see the error of his ways.

Then if the abusing spouse still won't change, the issue is brought to the leadership of the church in an effort to encourage repentance.

During this time of unrepentant abuse, the abused spouse may separate from the abuser. If the abusing spouse does not repent after being brought before the church leadership, then the abused spouse may treat the abuser as an unbeliever.

Here is where it gets tricky, because remember in 1 Corinthians 7, Paul said that if the unbelieving spouse wants to stay with the believing spouse, then the believing spouse should reciprocate. In a situation where the separation is caused by abuse, it would be hard to imagine that the abusing spouse would be celibate and separate.

This is where church leadership can provide the needed counsel and protection for the abused and develop a plan for reconciliation. As with all of us who feel ashamed, there is a tendency to isolate from people and shut down. However, both the abused and the abuser should put themselves under the authority of the church so that proper healing, discipline, and reconciliation can take place.

APPLICATION

- Drink deeply from Christian counsel. God gave believers the gift of Christian leadership to help couples work through these issues.

- Don't date a person that is abused, separated, and still married.

appendix:
STORIES AND
NOTES

I wanted to help further illustrate some of the principles found earlier in the common mistakes that we make because of the way things are. I placed those stories here, in the back of the book, so that you could have an easier time getting through the material. Some people find that stories get complicated, because they don't know the people. Others find illustrations make the principle come alive. So here is my attempt to help both parties.

I also stuck my notes back here just in case you are wanting to look up further information and see where I researched.

appendix: SINGLENESS

SOME THOUGHTS ON CHRISTIAN SINGLENESS
FROM ONE CALLED TO BE SINGLE

I have a suspicion that in modern Western Christendom, many or most Christians do not believe that the so-called "Gift of Singleness" actually exists.

Oh, they believe it in a sense. They believe that unmarried Christians exist; not to believe that would be, quite frankly, stupid. They may even believe that it is possible to be contentedly single, though I am convinced that not everyone does believe this; contented singles are often told that they "really do want to marry deep in their hearts", or they "just haven't found the right one yet". But what, I would argue, Christendom in general seems not to believe is that contented singleness is actually a gift.

Instead, I think that many Christians, probably on a mostly unconscious level (Paul's opinions on the subject are, after all, pretty hard to explain away), perceive contented singles as somehow defective. There is, they feel, something not quite right about us, something missing, something that ought to be functioning but isn't, as if we are romantic diabetics whose bodies do not produce something they ought to be producing. They feel, I think, much the same way they would feel (and rightly so) about a person who did not feel pain: it seems like a good thing, but it's actually a sign of real problems of some significance, and the most appropriate thing for the non-pain-feeling person to do would be to get to the doctor right away, to see if the problem could be put right. In the eyes of many Christians (and non-Christians as well), having no desire to marry is somehow pathological.

Even more damagingly, there is a definite tendency to suspect contented singles of being homosexual, possibly even homosexual without knowing it. I am fairly sure that if I ever do anything that will get historians discussing me after my death, at least some of them will insist that I was actually a closet lesbian all the time. And of course I can't really argue otherwise; someone will only say patronizingly that I "just haven't realized it yet", or I'm "still stuck in the closet", just as well-meaning people tell me that I'm "bound to find the right man eventually".

To this I can only say, "Bunk!" I would know better than they would. If my supposed homosexuality or desire to marry is so deeply buried that even I don't know about it, what difference does it make? If there really is anything buried that deep, it seems fairly irrelevant there. In the end, it comes down to this: I really do not have any interest at the moment in getting married, and I really do not have any interest in a same-sex romantic relationship either. You'll just have to take my word for it.

Where, then, does that leave us? I argue that contented Christian singleness does in fact exist; that there are people out there who are not just making the best of being unmarried when they want to marry, or who are not just trying to honor God by having homosexual feelings and choosing not to act upon them. I insist that people who genuinely wish to remain single are out there. But we return to the initial question: given the existence, and indeed the contentment, of such people, do they have an actual gift, or do they have a deficiency in their makeup?

It might be wise, first, to consider what we mean by gift. A gift is not a problem which brings positive results; the results might be a gift, but the problem itself is not. Patience developed through having an impossibly annoying coworker is a gift, but the annoyance itself, I would argue, is still an annoyance. A gift, in short, is a good thing, something that you can be happy to get. A person who wants to get married, but is single, does not generally have the gift of singleness, in my opinion. He or she might gain other gifts from this situation— patience, chastity, or healthy self-confidence, for instance—but the gift of singleness is probably not among them. The exception would be if the single person realizes that he or she actually wanted to get married in the first place only because it seemed the "usual" or "normal" thing to do; the news that he or she may remain happily single then comes as a delightful relief, a gift in the truest sense.

Similarly, a gift is not a deficiency, but rather something added on. If someone gives me a book as a birthday gift, I then have more reading matter than I did before. If there is a noisy cricket in my house, and someone finds it and throws it out as a gift, I have more peace and quiet than I did with the cricket there. If I have a gift for poetry or woodcarving or polo, I have talents added on, so that I have more than without them. Being blind, I would argue, is not a gift in itself in this sense; Fanny Crosby was grateful for her blindness, but she was grateful because of the great gifts she received through it, not, I would argue, because of the blindness in and of itself only. God's means of getting a gift to you is not a gift, any more than wrapping paper is. Similarly, if singleness can indeed properly be called a gift, it must make the person who has it more complete, not less.

According to this definition, is contented Christian singleness truly a gift? Yes, it is. It is not a negative thing though which, like wrapping paper, God can convey a positive good to us; neither is it a deficiency or lack, which can be used in mighty ways. To be sure, these are excellent things, and we have reason to be unceasingly grateful to God that He can and will bring good from evil. But they are not gifts in themselves; only what they produce are gifts.

Contented Christian singleness is a true gift. Those who have it are made more, not less; it is not something left out, but something added on.

Singleness brings blessing attainable in no other way. But what blessing? Paul has much to say on the subject in I Corinthians, chapter seven. In particular, he points out that being unmarried can lead to other beneficial types of singleness: singleness of mind, singleness of purpose, singleness of service, and singleness of focus. A married man, Paul explains, must be more worried about physical things than his unmarried brother, because he has more people to be responsible for (his wife and children) than only himself. Similarly, a married women must be concerned with her physical family and her spiritual one, whereas her unmarried sister is able to focus on the Church first, without conflict.

In short, as Paul says in verse 34, the interests of a married Christian are divided. He or she has more facets of life to appropriately balance, and potentially more conflicts to appropriately resolve; singleness avoids these complications. But it does more than simply avoid problems. It allows the single Christian to do the work of the Lord (whatever that might be in his or her own life) without the domestic distractions of a spouse and family. Whereas a married Christian must be balanced, a single Christian can instead be focused.

A single woman is able to mentor those younger or less mature, without balancing their needs with the needs of her own children. She is able to give time to the life of the church, without neglecting the life of her family. She can accept ministry opportunities without needing to consider the desires of her husband. She can give of her time, of her talents, of her skills, and of her money for the good of God's work, and do so with a singleness of focus impossible to a woman who also must balance the needs of her husband and family. Similarly, a single man is free to devote his time to service and God's work, without having to balance the need to devote time to his wife and children. He can council those in need, without worrying about neglecting to council his own children. He can help those in the body of Christ, without fear of leaving needs in his own household unattended to. He is able to go where God leads, without uprooting his family along with him. He can devote his time, abilities, and resources to God's work far more freely than a married man would be able to do.

Paul himself is not the only example of this, though he is a powerful one; there are other examples in scripture. For instance, in the second chapter of Luke, we find the story of Anna, an elderly prophetess who had been widowed for many years. She, we are told, never left the Temple complex, fasting and praying there continually. This would clearly have been impossible if she had had a husband and family to care for; she was permitted, by her singleness, to devote her undivided attention to God's work. And she was enabled by God to recognize the infant Christ when He was brought to the Temple, something which can only be regarded as an enviable honor.

So, then, am I arguing that singleness is superior to a married life? Certainly not. I do not believe that God accidentally appointed two men, one married (Peter) and one single (Paul), to be arguably the two mightiest of the apostles. "But each", as Paul says, "has his own gift from God, one person in this way and another in that way." (I Corinthians 7:7.) And he expands upon this later in the same letter, when he describes the Church as a body: "If the whole body were an eye, where would the hearing be? If the whole body were an ear, where would the sense of smell be? But now God has placed each one of the parts in one body just as He wanted. And if they were all the same part, where would the body be? Now there are many parts, yet one body. So the eye cannot say to the hand, 'I don't need you!' Or again, the head can't say to the feet, 'I don't need you!'" (12:17-21.) I might apply this to the current discussion by suggesting that the eye cannot dismiss the mouth because it is single, and the mouth cannot belittle the eye because it does not work properly without its mate! Both are exactly as they were designed to be, and both are necessary to the proper functioning of the whole body.

Imagine God as a builder, constructing a house. He uses a hammer to pound in nails; this hammer, in my metaphor, represents the married Christian. Like the hammer, married Christians have a particular design, and that design corresponds with what they are intended to accomplish in the Builder's work. The current perception has sometimes cast the single Christian in the role of a piece of broken cement or a rock, which the Builder will use if no hammer is

handy. It doesn't do the job very well, but it's better than nothing.

I might represent the single Christian as a screwdriver: it, like the hammer, is designed to do a specific task, which is different from the task of other tools. Neither tool can do the job of the other, at least not very well; but both belong to the same toolkit, both are effective in the Builder's hands, both are being used to construct the same house, and without both, the Builder's work would be hindered.

—Jennifer Paxton

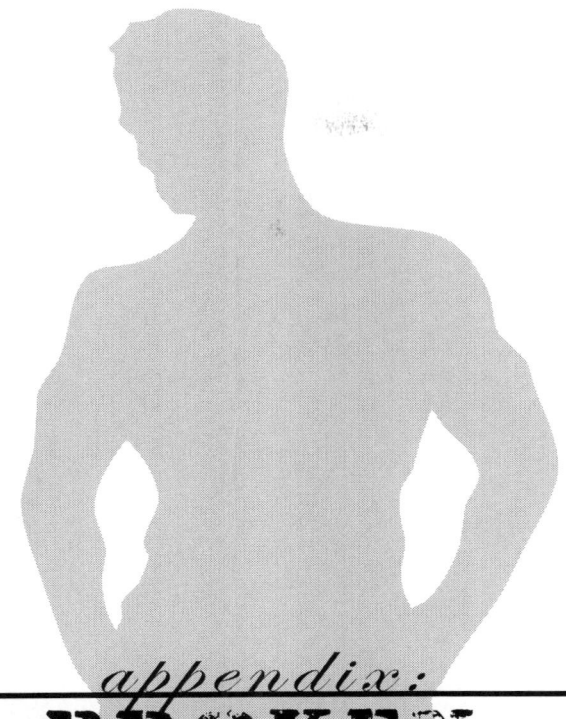

appendix:
BROKEN MARRIAGE

Jimmy grew up in a fairly well-to-do family. Dad had a great job in a western-wear corporate office. His mother was a stay-at-home mom. Initially, his parents' relationship was incredible. They had family dinners. They had family vacations. Dad came to all the little league games. Then things got complicated. Birthdays and Christmases became huge events, but dad was gone all the time.

Jimmy's father started to have little patience for his wife's lack of understanding of his need to be away. The arguments grew more intense, and he stayed away longer. In fact, when dad was home, he demeaned Jimmy's mother. He did it in a sarcastic kind of way. Every time his mom started to cry, he would console her by saying he was only joking.

Jimmy watched the way his father turned his mother into a woman walking on egg-shells. She was never sure how to act around him.

Eventually, a close friend of Jimmy had enough courage to tell him he was treating girlfriends in the same manner that his father had treated his mother before the divorce. Initially, Jimmy's anger caused him to shutdown. A week later, he realized his friend's comment was true and spoken in love.

"The way my dad treated my mom over the last 20 years taught me to treat women with no patience," Jimmy confided. "It taught me how to manipulate—how to get things my way."

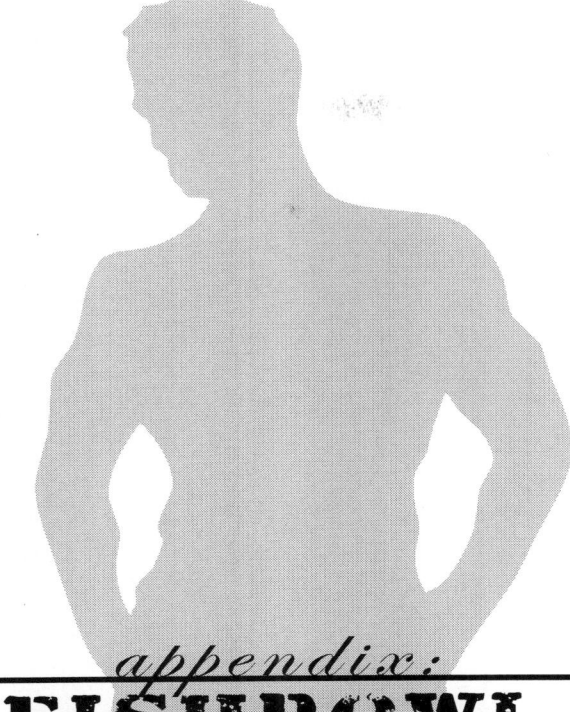

appendix: FISHBOWL

Jacob didn't have a chance with Erica, but he declared to "his community" how they were supposed to be together. At first everyone was cool with that, until it became clear to everyone that he didn't have a chance. Then Travis, being attracted to her character and looks, took an interest.

Jacob had her as marked territory, and it would break man-code for anyone of his friends to ask Erica out. Knowing this, Travis sought the approval of the group so that he could ask her out. Jacob was initially hurt by Travis moving in on his territory, but the community voted in favor of Travis and giving him a chance to date Erica.

Things got awkward at this point, and now Travis had to follow through on dating her. Even if he wasn't interested, he still had to date her for a couple months to show that his interest was more than surface deep.

Travis took Erica out on a group date first. In this group date, everyone knew the purpose was to chaperone Travis and Erica. Warren looking to accelerate the dating pace for Travis and Erica, pulled Erica aside to tell her how excited Travis was to be dating her—something Travis never said, but Warren thought he would help Travis out. It was fun to be around a newly dating couple.

Travis had fun, but he still wasn't sure. The group told him that he needed to go and meet the family if he wanted to really see what she was like. Travis decided to follow through on the advice and planned a trip to see her parents.

At this point they had been dating six months and the family was expecting a proposal; however, Travis felt like his hand was forced by those around him. He began to get cold feet. The trip to meet the parents went very well, but Travis began to feel increasingly pressured to make a decision. In his head, he wasn't sure if he really liked Erica, or if he liked the way the guys liked Erica.

The expectation of marriage caused Travis to end the relationship. He just couldn't take the pressure. He felt a little guilty for leading Erica on, but he just followed the advice of his community group who wanted to see Travis happy and felt Erica was the best fit.

Erica was hurt and angry towards Travis. Travis felt frustrated because he had so many opinions in his head. He had seen other guys in his group prolong relationships a year or two to "figure it out," ending the relationship with their "prime" behind them and the cost of using the "silver bullet" scarring the person's relationship capital within the fishbowl.

"I just didn't want to be stuck with someone that wasn't a fit, no matter how much everyone else wanted us to be together," Travis said.

The fishbowl was unkind to both Travis and Erica as rumors as to why they broke up filtered through their friends, acquaintances, and to finally people they hadn't met yet.

"It took months for me to feel comfortable even asking a different girl out. I felt black-balled by the system," Travis said.

Welcome to the fishbowl, Travis.

appendix:
SILVER BULLET

Charity and Jon dated off and on for their first two years of college. When it didn't work out, they had a tough time weaning off one another. In fact, they texted and communicated so much that once any guy got close to Charity, he would soon find that Charity spent a great deal of time texting Jon. He knew that she wasn't available emotionally and moved on.

Eventually Jon did move on. He dated a girl from another school. However his friendship with Charity never ended. They never had late night hang outs, but they kept the same circle of friends. Jon had the freedom to date other girls, but he made sure that Charity never could. When the gossip circled the Christian community at school, Charity was seen as marked territory. She had shot her silver bullet.

Only time away and perhaps a new circle of friends would rid of her marked status.

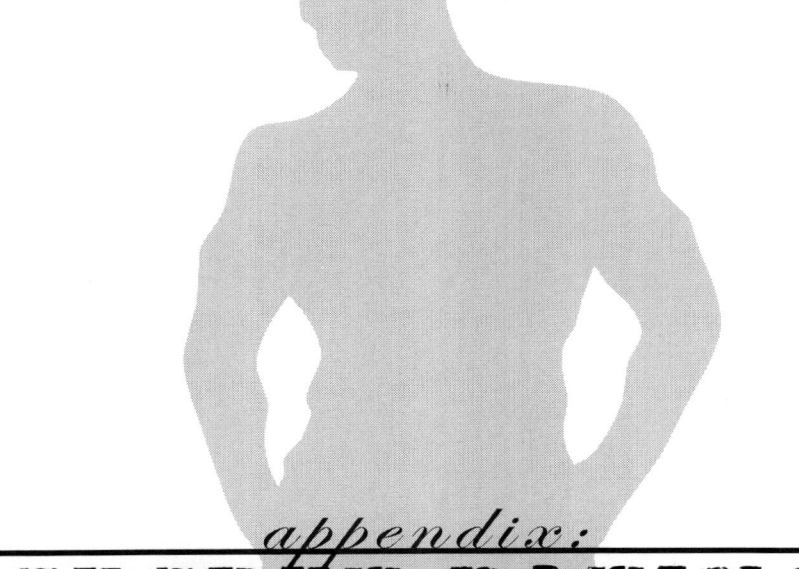

appendix:
SECRET DATING

Lisa and Jason were "just friends." They spent time together non-stop. Jason let people in on the fact they spent time together and was pretty clear with his closest friends that he was more than slightly interested. Lisa told everyone they were "just friends" and downplayed the amount of time they spent together. She said she was just like that with everyone.

Eventually, Jason realized he was in love with Lisa but wouldn't let her in on it for fear that she might not want to spend more time with him.

Lisa knew Jason was in love with her but couldn't admit it. She became dependent upon the affirmation, comfort, and attention she received from Jason. They enjoyed the company of one another and found themselves hanging out until 2am most nights. From Lisa's perspective, the relationship was equally plutonic. They were best friends. Lisa talked about the guy she wanted to marry, and it wasn't Jason. However, they spent so much time together, Jason started to believe he had a shot.

In Jason's eyes, there was an ever increasing mutual interest in a deeper, more committed, intimate relationship. One night, they had an especially sweet time together. Lisa shared some deeper emotional thoughts about her life. Jason enjoyed spending his late nights in her company. Without much thought, Jason's feelings took control as he leaned forward to kiss Lisa. Lisa, both flattered and surprised, locked lips with Jason for an hour and change.

The next day Lisa woke up feeling guilty for making out with a guy she only saw as a friend. She decided it wasn't a good idea to spend as much time with Jason and began to ignore some of his texts. Jason's feelings grew even stronger as he had now tasted the forbidden fruit and realized there was more than just a slim chance he could win Lisa.

Lisa, wanting to distance herself from Jason, started to get to know Jason's roommate, Daniel. She wanted to prove to Jason and everyone else that they were just friends. Daniel really liked Lisa, too. He liked that they shared intimate emotional feelings, thoughts, and especially spiritual opinions. Daniel and Lisa were both excited by this spiritual friendship they were forming. Lisa began to feel uncomfortable when she was with Daniel in front of Jason. It's not that she *liked* Jason. It's just that she really respected him. She wouldn't want Jason to think there was something happening between her and Daniel.

Jason and Daniel's relationship started to become a little complicated. It seemed that Daniel was now spending all of his time at someone else's house. Lisa was now ignoring all his texts. It wasn't like Jason had any claim on Lisa. Lisa and Daniel were "just friends," and no one needed to know their business.

Daniel and Lisa couldn't end their great conversations. They were so close emotionally that it didn't seemed right to not share physical closeness. Lisa enjoyed making out with Daniel. Her physical intimacy with Daniel didn't feel wrong like it did with Jason. She and Daniel had a spiritual connection. She believed there was really something happening in this friendship. They saw potential in one another. They decided that commitment should come when they knew for sure. Right then, it was better not to be seen as a "couple."

Many nights of accidently making-out passed. The semester ended. Most people went home and visited family. Lisa and Daniel hadn't left for break yet, because they wanted a few more days together.

One night, the heat of their physical intensity led to sex. Before Daniel knew what happened, Lisa was out of his house and ignoring all his calls. Lisa returned home plagued by guilt. She decided it was best to break things off with Daniel. She never intended to have sex with someone until her wedding night.

Lisa began to miss the respect Jason had for her. He managed to control himself more than Daniel. This *must be* God leading her back to Jason.

In the meantime, Daniel started talking more to Lisa's friend Emily. Emily was aware that *something* happened with Lisa and Daniel. Emily was unwilling to simply hang out with Daniel. She let him know she would only spend time together if they could make it public and called their hang-outs "dates."

Daniel really liked Emily and said he was willing to comply with her requests. Part of making their dating public meant Daniel must talk with Emily's dad and mentor on the phone during their dating relationship.

Daniel, once again, complied with Emily's request. During Daniel and Emily's dating relationship, both received counsel and advice from older people and peers. About 2 months in, they decided it was probably not the best idea to move forward.

They hadn't kissed yet, so returning back to the friendship they had all of college was no big deal. It required a little discipline for them not to talk for one week, and then all became normal again.

Meanwhile Lisa and Jason are back to their hidden hang-out-make-out "friendship." About 6 months later, Jason found out about the intimacy Lisa and Daniel shared in the previous semester. He felt humiliated and hurt. He did all he could to distance himself from them. Lisa felt really bad for Jason and intensely missed his company, affirmation and attention.

She texted, called and sent sweet notes to Jason. Jason was determined not to cave. He resisted text message after text message. But he was only human. When he moved back to school to start another semester, he felt all the chemistry he once had with Lisa. The two agreed to date this time, but they only wanted it to be "official" in private. They didn't want it to be public, because Jason didn't want to be ridiculed by his parents who saw how hurt Jason was. Lisa didn't want to come across as the promiscuous woman who used people.

Not long after their secret dating time, Lisa realized she didn't actually want to be with Jason at all. She wanted the attention. In fact, the thought of a long-term intimate relationship with him caused her to cringe. So for the fourth or fifth time, we've lost count by now, Lisa broke Jason's heart.

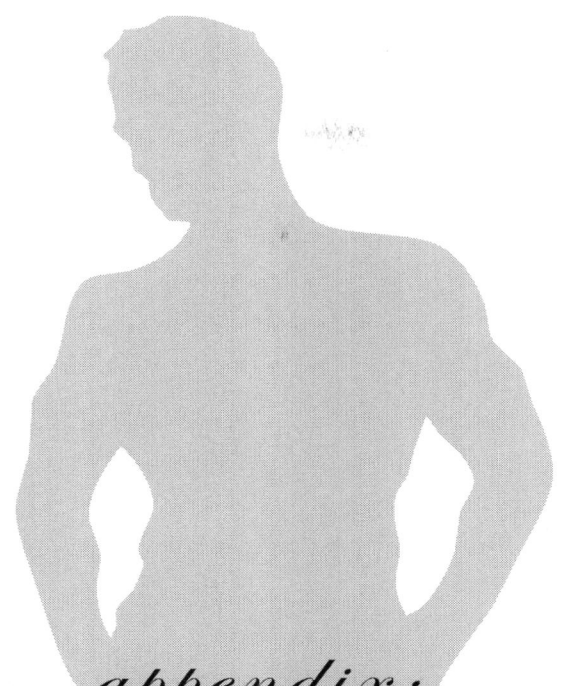

appendix: EMOTIONAL DUMPING

Chrissy and George went to Passion with a group from their university. The excitement of Crowder, Tomlin, Redman, Stanfill, and Hillsong United was electric even before they left town with their college pastor at the helm of their 15-passenger van for Atlanta.

George, a sophomore transfer, started scanning iTunes, hoping that a new release would accompany Passion. Chrissy asked Audrey for advice concerning some of the high school girls she had been mentoring that semester. After a 12-hour trip, they arrived ready to experience the worship and hear Louie Giglio and Beth Moore talk.

As they walked out of the Phillips Arena, George pulled Chrissy aside.

"Hey, I overheard that you mentor some high school kids. Are you having drama?"

Chrissy smiled. "Yeah, a lot. These girls are 16 going on 35 with a mid-life crisis."

George and Chrissy sat down outside the prayer room of the conference and started talking about their experiences with high school ministry. Then George, interested in Chrissy, started to ask deeper questions about how she came to faith.

"Well," Chrissy started, excited to retell her story of faith, "I grew up in a home where my father was abusive. He's a great guy and all when he is sober, but the drinking made him crazy."

"No way," George said. "Me too, but just a little different. My dad was never around. I always felt lonely like no one understood me."

"Me too," Chrissy said. "I think that is why I have always struggled physically with guys. I just want someone to get me."

"Me too." George said. He couldn't believe how similar Chrissy and he were. He started to feel like this could be *the one*. He was talking to the female version of himself.

George and Chrissy skipped on the John Piper session and continued to hang out by the prayer room. They talked about their parents and their dreams to be missionaries to the Dalite people of India. Chrissy had her head on George's shoulder and shared with him that no one ever understood her like him. George felt the same way. At around 3am, they decided to head back to their hotel room to get some sleep before the 9am break out group started.

Chrissy got back to her room surprised to see several other girls still up talking.

"Where have you been?" Audrey asked.

"Just hanging out by the prayer room," Chrissy answered.

"Oh cool," Audrey said and then the conversation went back to Beth Moore's talk.

The next morning, George found Chrissy and they were inseparable for the entire day. That night Hillsong led worship and both George and Chrissy felt tingles as they lifted their hands to the Lord.

George, with eyes closed, "accidentally" touched Chrissy's raised hand. Her tingles became shivers, and she couldn't wait for another late night talk.

After the Hillsong concert ended, George and Chrissy went for a walk around the Georgia World Congress Center to talk about how amazing God was that night and to get to know each other a little better. They sat down on the curb and shared how far they'd gone sexually. Chrissy was impressed that George hadn't gone all the way yet. She felt slightly guilty that she had. George reminded her of God's grace, and she started to cry.

With tears streaming down her face, she buried her head into his shoulder.

"Do you think anyone will still love me?" she asked.

"Jesus still loves you, and I think you are amazing," George said.

George lifted her head off his shoulder and looked her in the eye, "You are beautiful."

She looked away and then he lifted her chin and kissed her. They kissed for a while and went back to their hotel rooms at 3am.

The next night they crossed physical boundaries and left Passion feeling guilty. Overwhelmed with guilt, Chrissy kept calling George. However, George would only respond with one word texts. He understood he was forgiven and couldn't understand why Chrissy was making such a big deal about all this. Finally, he labeled her as "Needy" and stopped responding to her completely.

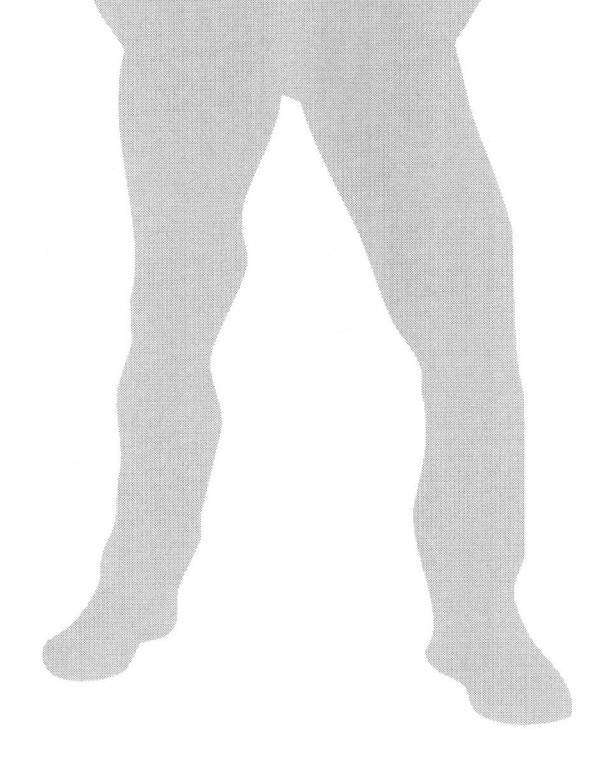

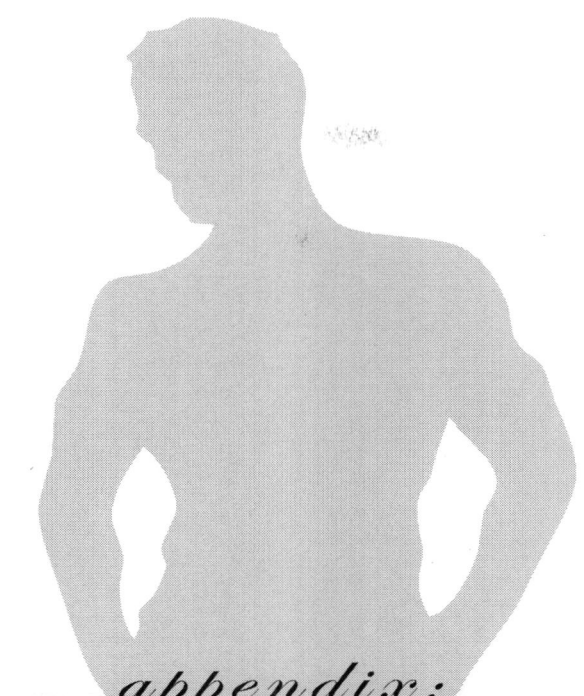

appendix: MISSIONARY DATER

Rachel finished college single with several great guy friends, but no one interested. Frustrated, she decided to date a guy who didn't believe in Jesus but was open to spiritual things. At first, her boyfriend, Jordan, had no problem going to church. But when the pastor kept talking about no sex before marriage, he got a little uncomfortable.

He started to make excuses for not going to church. Rachel soon became frustrated that they could not have any spiritual conversations but just felt that she needed to be the light in his dark world. Who else would tell him about Jesus?

The trouble was she didn't tell him about Jesus either. It wasn't until a local ministry needed her help at a retreat that she got Jordan to come. She was shocked to find out through the discussions that Jordan had with some of the guys that he not only wasn't into Jesus, but he was skeptical about the whole "ponzi-scheme" of Christianity.

Rachel was grateful that he was open about where he was spiritually, but she wasn't sure he would ever come around. She was conflicted because she was so emotionally invested in Jordan's life. How could she let him down like that and make something like faith come between them? She decided she wouldn't marry him until he was a believer, but she wouldn't break it off either.

Rachel continues to date him in an awkward guilt-filled relationship where sex has become something that Rachel has to get over in hopes that one day he will pop the question.

appendix:
VOICE OF GOD
DATER

Stephanie dated a guy, Michael, for two months. She would often confide to Adrienne and other confidants of her liking Michael. When they started dating, Stephanie felt the relationship pick up speed and quickly told others her excitement. Unfortunately, Michael didn't feel the same. He kept himself busy and called her up around 11pm when he felt lonely.

Michael knew they shouldn't continue seeing each other but didn't want to hurt her feelings. Thankfully, he still had the "Voice of God" card to play. She had borrowed CDs. He decided that if Stephanie gave him back the CDs then that was God saying they should break up.

Stephanie, being a normal responsible person, gave him back the CDs. Once the CDs were in his hand, a sense of freedom enveloped Michael.

"Stephanie," he started, his face changing, "God has spoken. I can't date you anymore."

Michael proceeded to explain to confused Stephanie of how God spoke through her returning the CDs. How could Stephanie argue with that? Satisfied, Michael turned to go leaving Stephanie bewildered double checking her relationship with God.

Thankfully, Stephanie is no idiot. Her heartbreak lasted long enough for her to tell the story to someone else and get a good laugh out of it.

Here's the reality. Michael lacked the capacity to explain he wasn't interested. The end result is that another person claiming the "Voice of God" is discredited, and Christians are seen as "quacks" playing the God card to evade real conflict.

I have talked with hundreds of people about this. I've found that there are some who have had legitimate "Voice of God" type things happen. They felt God speak to them about a person, and then they ended up marrying them.

However, if God tells you something about a particular love interest, then is He not capable of carrying it through to marriage? How could God be sovereign if He told you to marry someone, and you somehow botched it. Even with you completely screwing it up, God could still change her heart to marry you.

Remember, this isn't about capturing *the one* that might get away, but rather becoming *the one* God has called you to be.

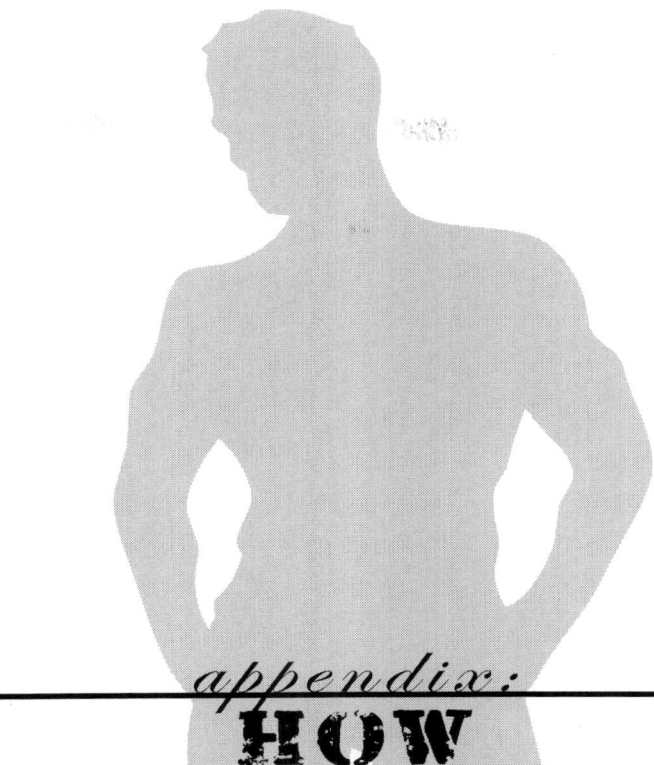

appendix:
HOW

Scott sat frazzled and stared at the door. Kathryn had just walked out in a rage. It was over and now Scott had some serious thinking to do.

He never thought of himself as having a problem. Sure he had some porn on his computer, but he didn't look at it every day. How Kathryn found it while googling places to go for dinner, he didn't know. But she had and, in a moment, she left. This time for good.

Scott didn't feel like calling anyone or telling anyone. He went through his porn for one last look. He promised himself he would delete every file on the computer, but he couldn't. A week later, he finally did.

Porn offered him something that Kathryn or any other woman he knew, for that matter, never could. Porn offered him power. He couldn't be rejected. He could live out a god-like status. It was a great escape from an otherwise disappointing life.

At first he thought Kathryn was the problem. She held a holier than thou standard that caused him to live in hiding from her. She always was pushing him to get involved in a Bible study or church or something, but every time he went, he felt that if anyone knew he struggled, he would be rejected again.

Scott went through his DVD collection and pulled out several seasons of Seinfeld. It took him a week to recalibrate from Kathryn and porn to killing terrorists and saving the world. He then made a life-altering decision. He'd check out one of those Celebrate Recovery things that Kathryn had mentioned she had at her church. She told him just about every church in Dallas had one, so he committed to go.

The first week was easy. He listened to some guy talk about his struggle with porn and how he overcame it through Celebrate Recovery groups. After that, he was put with three other first timers. His hands started to sweat as Nate, the leader, asked him why he was there. Scott hated going first, but did his best in being authentic. He explained his issue, which really wasn't that big of a deal, and then he told them about Kathryn, and how he'd taken the last week off work to explore his depression and was now ready for help. Nate didn't judge, just told him that he was grateful Scott chose to come. The other guys told their stories. One talked about his battle with Oxycotton, and the other shared his struggle with eating. Apparently, he felt he had an addiction to Jason's Deli. Scott wasn't sold on this thing dubbed CR, but he decided to come back again.

The next couple weeks of interacting in a big group and sharing all their struggles seemed redundant. Scott listened to the Jason's Deli guy go on and on about how he thought about Jason's Deli. Scott did his best to keep a straight face.

When it was his turn, he talked about porn. He talked about the lonliness. He had never shared his fear of rejection out loud with anyone. It was sort of therapeutic. He hoped to God he didn't sound like the Jason's Deli guy, but after a couple of weeks of going through the program, he didn't care about sharing intimately. In fact, he came to see that the Jason's Deli guy had the same issue he had—something had become greater than Jesus.

Scott moved from the big group to a smaller group and the Jason's Deli guy along with four others joined him. There they learned together strategies for defeating idolatry.

In Scott's engineering classes back in college, he had learned to do tough mathematical formulas and equations by doing a lot of practice problems. He knew that if he practiced it enough, he would learn the different nuances of engineering and then could implement the right strategy needed to solve that problem.

It felt that the same formula applied to breaking him free from his addiction. Scott didn't like that word, but he went with it, because he didn't have anything better. He just thought that if he was a new creation, then the old things would pass away. Well, apparently the urges hadn't, and he would worry about the theology later.

Whenever the urge to look at porn came he started to implement what the folks in his small group taught him. His first job was to call his small group leader. Second, he would pray with him or another accountability partner. Third, he would recite the scripture he memorized for whatever dysfunctional pattern that He was trying to get Jesus to renew. Finally, he invited Jesus into his sin to cleanse it.

It felt weird telling people who hadn't gone through it about it, so he didn't. He had also committed to not date through this process. Scott was so broken he didn't care about that, but other guys in the group shared how they struggled not to date. At first Scott looked at them like he first looked at the Jason's Deli guy, but eventually God gave him compassion for them and he listened to their struggles.

They met regularly for a year. They developed positive ways to deal with lonliness and rejection. They learned to involve other Christians in their struggles. Finally, even Scott felt ready to date again.

He decided to call Kathryn. It took everything in him to look her up on Facebook. He was just grateful there wasn't a profile pic of her with another guy. We he got her number, he dialed it on his iPhone, and then stared at it. After a minute of debate, he hit call.

Kathryn answered, but she wasn't interested. The conversation lasted only 48 seconds. Scott wasn't prepared for outright rejection. He spiraled and felt the same way he did a year ago. He went to his computer and then thought twice about it and drove to Katy Trail and went for a walk. He called several guys in his Recovery Group, hoping none of them would answer so he might have an excuse to go find an internet fantasy, but the Jason's Deli guy answered on the first ring.

"What's up Scott?" He asked.

"Rejection," Scott said, and he explained what happened. Through prayer, scripture, and the presence of a friend, Scott made it through the night without porn and without going into despair.

Scott recently started dating again. He knows how to run from porn. He has friends supporting him, and he knows who to run to if the rejection comes again.

appendix: GIVE ME STEPS

Luke never had parents that involved themselves in his life. It wasn't that they didn't love him, but both parents worked and had high expectations for Luke. This left Luke longing for relationship. In High School, Luke focused solely on school trying as hard as he could to please his parents. He graduated top ten and soon found himself going to TCU on a full ride. At TCU, his attention turned from pleasing his parents to pleasing women. He never considered himself promiscuous. Oral sex wasn't really that bad, he thought. There was no chance of pregnancy, abortion, or most STDs. He found that giving girls attention created in them a need for him. He fed on it.

However, he found that the girls he dated or "hung out" with didn't have what he wanted in a wife. He became a Christian his junior year, but in all reality there was a disconnect between his spiritual life and the way he viewed women. He heard a sermon that hit him square in the jaw. When women replace God as your sole source of joy, you are in idolatry. Luke wasn't sure if his search for a relationship was his sole source of joy, but he couldn't deny that he surfed through his friends through social media looking for potential mates. He usually went off the hot profile pic and then started sifting through their interests.

While watching Monday night football, his roommate, Bryan, looked over at him. "Dude, whose profile you checking out?"

Luke looked at the name for the first time and said, "Melissa Thornburg, you know her?"

"No, do you?"

"No."

"Then why are you on her profile?"

"Just checking her out?"

"Why?"

"I don't know, you know? Maybe she's a good match." As soon as Luke said that, he knew it sounded dumb.

"Bro, when you look at chicks based on what status they give you, you are setting yourself up for pain," Bryan said.

"What do you mean?" Luke asked.

"Well, I've been glancing at your Facebook during commercials and noticing you going through their pics. You friended thirty girls in the past two hours and not one of them is anyone you or I know. Even if you get to know one of these girls, you view them as a piece of meat and not as a sister," Bryan said.

"So? Don't you want to be attracted to your wife?" Luke asked.

"Yeah, but when you start from the hot factor, you miss out on a ton of girls who are quality and are not wearing stilettos and halter tops for all the world to see."

"That's easy for you to say, your girlfriend is hot," Luke said.

"Yeah, well, no matter how hot she is, there's always a girl hotter. And if she is putting out pics of her hotness all the time, then how much time is she cultivating her relationship with God?"

"Bro, seriously, I'm not looking for an Amish girl."

"Neither am I, Kelsey isn't exactly Amish," Bryan said.

"Yeah and she does wear stilettos," Luke reminded Bryan.

"True, but I met her serving at church when she wore flats, jeans, and a sweatshirt."

"Okay, Mr. Holy. I'm not quite like that. I'm sorry, if I view women as hotties, and you view them as sisters."

"Well, who has the hottie, and who doesn't?" Bryan chided.

"Touché. Okay, fine, let's see what happens if I trust God to change me to look at women like you do. I know I shouldn't expect a magic spell to happen and a hottie..."

"A woman," Bryan corrected.

"Fine, I'll trust God to change me to look at women as sisters."

"Good, I'll hold you to it," Bryan said.

The first week was hard for Luke. He had to deactivate his Facebook account, because the temptation became too strong. He settled for updating Twitter from his smart phone instead. After two weeks, he forgot about checking out women on the internet and started working on viewing women as sisters at church. That seemed a bit difficult at first. He decided to volunteer for the greeting team. He found that when he worked with women on a regular basis, he didn't view them as hot at all.

"Okay, this is weird," Luke confided in Bryan. "All the girls I used to fantasize about, I no longer fantasize about cause I know them."

"Exactly."

"Yeah, but how am I going to ever be attracted to a girl if I know them too well?" Luke asked. Bryan gave Luke a smirk. "Okay, that does sounds dumb."

"Yeah it does, but retraining your mind to look at women from God's perspective, instead of your private's perspective takes a little time."

"I'm waiting," Luke said. "I'm just not sure if it will ever happen."

"Patience can't be microwaved," Bryan said.

"You have a line for everything."

Over time, Luke retrained his mind. Some days he felt it tougher to retrain his mind than it did to rehab his knee after ACL surgery in college. Today, he has expanded his circle of friends to include women. He has found moments of attraction to some of them. The renewing the mind thing takes time. All that know Luke are confident he is on the right path.

appendix:
NOTES

1. Chapter One: Commentary on Ezer from the NET Bible.

2. Chapter One: Commentary on Helper from M. L. Rosenzweig, "A Helper Equal to Him," Jud 139 (1986): 277-80.

3. Chapter Two: I extensively used Dr. Constable Notes on Deuteronomy from Soniclight.com accessed November 2011

4. Chapter Three: Commentary of G. D. Fee, "1 Corinthians 7:1 in the NIV," JETS 23 (1980): 307-14.
   "It is good for a man not to touch a woman," a euphemism for sexual relations. This idiom occurs ten times in Greek literature, and all of the references except one appear to refer to sexual relations (cf., e.g., Josephus, Ant. 1.8.1 [1.163]; Gen 20:6 [LXX]; Prov 6:29

[LXX]). For discussion see G. D. Fee, First Corinthians (NICNT), 275. Many recent interpreters believe that here again (as in 6:12–13) Paul cites a slogan the Corinthians apparently used to justify their actions. If this is so, Paul agrees with the slogan in part, but corrects it in the following verses to show how the Corinthians misused the idea to justify abstinence within marriage (cf. 8:1, 4; 10:23). See also

5. Chapter Three: I extensively used Dr. Constable Notes on 1 Corinthians from Soniclight.com accessed March 2011

6. Chapter Three: Gary Thomas, *Sacred Marriage*

7. Chapter Five: All facts from this chapter are taken from this website http://www.buzzle.com/articles/divorce-rate-in-america.html on August 8, 2011.

8. Chapter Eleven: I owe all I know about Ruth and Boaz from my professor Dr. Robert Chisholm and the classes that I took at Dallas Theological Seminary. His commentary on Ruth is unbelievable.

9. Chapter Thirteen: NET Bible Notes from Song of Solomon 1:4.
    The verb (mashakh, "draw") is a figurative expression (hypocatastasis) which draws an implied comparison between the physical acting of leading a person with the romantic action of leading a person in love. Elsewhere it is used figuratively of a master gently leading an animal with leather cords (Hos 11:4) and of a military victor leading his captives (Jer 31:3). The point of comparison might be that the woman wants to be the willing captive of the love of her beloved, that is, a willing prisoner of his love.

10. Chapter Thirteen: I again used Dr. Constable's notes on Song of Solomon accessed June 2011

11. Chapter Thirteen: I used *The Book of Romance: What Solomon Says About Love, Sex, and Intimacy*, 2007 by Tommy Nelson extensively here.

12. Chapter Thirteen: I used Dr. Constable's notes on Song of Solomon page 15 from www.soniclight.com accessed June 2011

13. Chapter Fifteen: I used Dr. Constable's notes on Proverbs from www.soniclight.com accessed July 2011.

14. Chapter Nineteen: My church Watermark Community Church provided me all the information and insight on dating for the divorced. They would never advocate divorce, but rather reconciliation. Their position has been to error on the side of grace for those who are in the difficult position of being divorced

15419574R00104

Made in the USA
Charleston, SC
02 November 2012